Pocket Guide
to Men

Contents

Contents

Introduction

In the old days, when men were men and women made the tea, relationships were much less complicated. Everyone knew the rules and, on the whole, obeyed them. But now everything's changed – women are out there, hustling and bustling, wheeling and dealing, and men are . . . well, trying to compete. So now that we're playing a different game it looks like we both need some help negotiating the minefield of modern relationships, and this little **Guide** is just the thing. Specially designed to help women understand more about men (and men more about themselves), it starts at the very beginning with the basic **Things You Should Know . . .** and **What Men are Like . . .** both required reading before you even consider embarking on a relationship.

Now fully equipped to launch yourself into the dating game, **A Guide to Chat-up Lines** lists the good, the bad and the downright dodgy – plus a few for you to try yourself. Once you've got your man it is essential that he understands and learns the **New Rules** for keeping you happy and maintaining a successful relationship. A reminder of the **Old Rules** *(which no longer apply)* is also included just in case he confuses them.

Of course, even when men try *really* hard misunderstandings will sometimes arise and Chapter 5, **Understanding What he Says**, is dedicated to helping you avoid or resolve these by decoding and analysing what men say and what they actually mean. And when it all goes wrong, as sometimes it does, there's nothing better than some **Sweet Revenge**. Enjoy jokes at his expense, strike terror into his heart by asking him the five most feared questions known to man and stock up on biting responses to his sarcastic comments. And, when all else fails, abandon him altogether – buy a dog or take up a new hobby. Until the next time . . .

CHAPTER 1

Things You Should Know . . .

Look before you leap is always wise advice – and never more so than with regard to men. So, if you're actually seriously thinking of becoming involved with a man, there are certain features of the breed you should be aware of before you start. The following section will give you the basic facts – after that the decision is yours . . .

The Complex Man

Most men are halfway through life before they realize it's a "do-it-yourself" thing.

A man will pay £2 for a £1 item he needs.
A woman will pay £1 for a £2 item she doesn't need.

No man has ever seen the movie *The Way We Were* twice voluntarily.

What separates the men from the boys is the size of their toys.

Lateness provides a legitimate excuse for a man to drive like a maniac.

A man is one who loses his illusions first, his teeth second, and his follies last.

Most women are introspective: "Am I in love?" "Am I creatively fulfilled?"
Most men are outrospective: "Did my team win?" "How's my car?"

Only a man would buy a £500 car and put a £4000 stereo in it.

No man is charming all the time – even Cary Grant is on record saying he wished he could be Cary Grant.

If a man were presented with a device that could cure all disease, wipe out world hunger and eliminate war and violence world-wide, his first instinct would be to take it apart.

All men would still really like to own a train set.

Homo Domesticus

Man's greatest achievement was the invention of the remote control.

You know a man's planning for the future when he buys two cases of beer instead of one.

Men usually sort their laundry into "Filthy" and "Filthy but Wearable".

Men rarely call the Home Shopping Network.

You know you're in a bachelor pad when all the house plants are dead and there's something huge growing in the fridge.

The Male Ego

A man likes a phone with lots of buttons. It makes him feel important.

Men don't get lost: they are only exploring alternative destinations.

Men are sensitive in strange ways. If a man has built a fire and the last log does not burn, he will take it personally.

Men must be the first to read the newpaper in the morning. Not being the first is upsetting to their psyches.

Men are self-confident because they grow up identifying with super-heroes. Women have bad self-images because they grow up identifying with Barbie.

When a man says "I'm not lost – I know exactly where we are', start wondering if anyone will ever see you alive again.

Why don't men get PMS? What would be the point? They act like that all the time.

The way a man looks at himself in a mirror will tell you if he can ever care about anyone else.

Never trust a man who says he's the boss at home – he'll most likely lie about other things as well.

Men view life as a competition: if you're better at something than they are, they'll pretend it's not important.

Don't try to teach men how to do anything in public. They can, however, be taught in private.

Be careful of men who are bald and rich: the arrogance of "rich" usually cancels out the nice of "bald".

Moses wandered in the desert for 40 years because he refused to ask directions.

Men love watches with multiple functions, for example, one that is also a combination address book, Swiss Army knife and piano.

Men and Sex

Sleeping with a man is like a soap opera: just when it's getting interesting, they're finished until next time.

An erection is like the Theory of Relativity – the more you think about it, the harder it gets.

A man's idea of safe sex is a padded headboard.

Sex alleviates tension. Love causes it.

How to satisfy a man every time: show up naked, with beer.

Women fake orgasms because men fake foreplay.

Sex without love is an empty experience. But as far as empty experiences go, it's one of the best.

If God had meant us to have group sex, he'd have given us more organs.

Men were given larger brains than dogs so they wouldn't hump women's legs at cocktail parties.

If sex is so personal, why do we have to share it with someone?

A single man in his forties often has a problem finding women at his level of maturity. That's why he dates someone half his age.

Men and sperm have something in common: both have a one-in-a-million chance of becoming a human being.

God blessed men with a penis and a brain – the problem is that He only gave them enough blood to operate one organ at a time.

You can tell a man is sexually excited if he's breathing.

Foreplay for a man is half an hour of begging.

There are only two four-letter words that are offensive to men – "don't" and "stop" (unless they're used together).

Women need a reason to have sex – men just need a place.

Men allow their sex instincts to drive them where their intelligence would never take them.

If a man is writhing on your bed, gasping for air and calling your name, you didn't hold the pillow over his face for long enough.

A man who boasts of reading the classics has been subscribing to *Playboy* since 1972.

If a woman thinks the way to a man's heart is through his stomach, she's aiming too high.

A man is like a snowstorm: you don't know when he's coming, how many inches you'll get, or how long it'll stay.

Men and Love

When a man falls in love, he wants to go to bed. When a woman falls in love, she wants to talk about it.

The perfect lover is one who turns into a pizza at 4 a.m.

Men fall in love at first sight because it saves a lot of time.

If you love someone, let her go. If she comes back, great. If not, she's probably having dinner with someone more attractive than you.

Love is the delightful interval between meeting a beautiful girl and discovering that she looks like a haddock.

Love is the delusion that one man differs from another.

Every man knows that somewhere in the universe exists his perfect soulmate – but looking for her is much more difficult than just staying at home and ordering another pizza.

Men always want to be a woman's first love. Women want to be a man's last romance.

A man's idea of honesty in a relationship is telling you his real name.

If it's a serious relationship, he likes you more than his truck.

Men and the Opposite Sex

If a man says something in a forest and there are no women present, he is still wrong.

Bachelors know more about women than married men. If they didn't, they'd be married too.

Diamonds are a girl's best friend. Dogs are man's best friend. Which is the dumber sex?

God made man before woman to give him time to think of an answer to her first question.

In the beginning, God created earth and rested. Then God created man and rested. Then God created woman. Since then, neither God nor man has rested.

A man who won't lie to a woman has very little consideration for her feelings.

A bachelor is a man who never makes the same mistake once.

The most important thing in a relationship between a man and a woman is that one of them be good at taking orders.

A man who is old enough to know better is always on the look-out for a girl who doesn't.

Men are like games: you play with them constantly, then when you're sick of them you give them away.

A man who has everything needs a woman to show him how to work it.

Man's greatest advantage in the battle of the sexes is woman's curiosity.

A woman has the last word in any argument. Anything a man says after that is the beginning of a new argument.

Men are like animals, but they make great pets.

Women need more imagination than men, in order to be able to tell men how wonderful they are.

There are men who are sensitive, caring and good-looking, but they probably already have boyfriends.

When women are depressed they eat or go shopping. Men invade another country.

Men have higher body temperatures than women. If your central heating packs in, sleep next to a man. They are like portable heaters that snore.

To a man, a kiss is just an application for a better position.

It's not true that men prefer foolish women. They prefer women who can simulate foolishness whenever necessary, which is the very core of intelligence.

If a man appears sexy, caring and smart, give him a day or two and he'll be back to his usual self.

When women go through the menopause, they gain weight and get hot flushes.
When men go through the menopause, they date young girls and drive motorcycles.

Men and Marriage

Men would like monogamy better if it sounded less like monotony.

A lot of men define marriage as a way to get maid service for free.

A woman worries about the future until she gets a husband. A man never worries about the future until he gets a wife.

The difference between a new husband and a new dog is that after a year, the dog is still excited to see you.

Marriage is a wonderful invention; but, then again, so is a bicycle repair kit.

Love is an obsessive delusion that is cured by marriage.

A man in love is incomplete until he is married. Then he is finished.

Only two things are necessary to keep one's wife happy. One is to let her think she is having her own way, and the other is to let her have it.

Adam and Eve had an ideal marriage. He didn't have to hear about all the men she could have married, and she didn't have to hear about how well his mother cooked.

A husband is what is left of the lover after the nerve has been extracted.

They say 50 per cent of all marriages end in divorce. That's not as bad as it sounds, considering that the other 50 per cent end in death.

By all means marry. If you get a good wife, you'll be happy. If you get a bad one, you'll become a philosopher.

Husbands are like fires: they go out when unattended.

When a man steals your wife, there is no better revenge than to let him keep her.

Mahatma Gandhi was what wives wish their husbands were: thin, tan and moral.

Many a man owes his success to his first wife, and his second wife to his success.

Marriage is the triumph of imagination over intelligence.
Re-marriage is the triumph of hope over experience.

Men marry because they are tired; women marry because
they are curious – both are disappointed.

Some husbands are living proof that a woman can take a
joke.

Husbands are like cars: all are good the first year.

When a husband brings his wife flowers for no reason –
there's a reason.

It is never okay to throw away veteran underwear: if your wife tries to throw away your underwear, she is jealous, because you have a more intimate relationship with your pants than with her.

If a man opens the door of his car for his wife, either the car is new, or the wife.

There are two times when a man doesn't understand a woman: before marriage and after marriage.

When sending your wife down the road with a petrol can, it is impolite to ask her to bring back beer.

Single women complain that all the good men are married, while all married women complain about their lousy husbands. This confirms that there is no such thing as a good man.

The honeymoon is over when you start to go out with the boys on Wednesday nights, and so does she.

A successful man is one who makes more money than his wife can spend.

Married men live longer than single men, but married men are a lot more willing to die.

Husbands are like children – they're fine if they're somebody else's.

The only "women's work" that is never done is the stuff a wife asks her husband to do.

Do not argue with a wife who is packing your parachute.

Any married man should forget his mistakes. There's no use in two people remembering the same thing.

Before marriage, a man will lie awake all night thinking about something his lover said. After marriage, he'll fall asleep before his wife finishes . . . brushing her teeth.

Men get married so they don't have to hold their stomachs in any more.

If you meet a man who would make a good husband, chances are he already is.

Getting married is like going to a restaurant with friends – you order what you want, then when you see what the other person has, you wish you ordered that.

A husband who says "We don't need material goods to prove our love" has forgotten your anniversary.

If it weren't for marriage, men would go through life thinking they had no faults at all.

A man marries a women expecting that she won't change, but she does.
A woman marries a man expecting he will change, but he doesn't.

For most men, the most effective way to remember their wife's birthday is to forget it once.

Many husbands are like old lawnmowers – they're hard to get started, emit noxious odours and half the time don't work.

Marrying a divorced man is ecologically responsible. In a world where there are more women than men, it pays to recycle.

Men and Style

Men who have pierced ears are better prepared for marriage. They have experienced pain and have bought jewellery.

All men are afraid of eyelash curlers – keep one under your pillow, instead of a gun.

A good place to meet a man is at the dry cleaner's – these men usually have jobs and they bathe.

Men have an easier time than women when buying bathing suits. There are two types for women: depressing and more depressing. And two types for men: nerdy and not nerdy.

Most men hate to shop – that's why the men's department is usually on the first floor of a department store, three feet from the door.

Short skirts have a tendency to make men polite. Have you ever seen a man get on a bus ahead of a woman wearing a short skirt?

A man who can dress himself without looking ridiculous is probably gay.

You will never see a man walk into a party and say "Oh my God, get me out of here. I'm so embarrassed – there's another man wearing a black tuxedo."

When out shopping, if a man tells his girlfriend she looks terrific in that outfit, he's starving.

Men wake up as good-looking as they went to bed. Women somehow deteriorate during the night.

Men who are going bald often wear baseball caps.

Men are brave enough to go to war, but not brave enough to get a bikini wax.

If men can run the world, why can't they stop wearing neckties? How intelligent is it to start the day by tying a little noose around your neck?

Men don't get cellulite – many women believe that, for this reason alone, God might just be a male.

When a woman finds her favourite dress is too tight, she's gained weight.
When a man finds his favourite trousers are too tight, they've shrunk in the wash.

Men who listen to classical music tend not to spit.

Men mismatch their clothes so women will think they don't have a girlfriend.

Men and the Kitchen

Men are good at the barbeque – they like to cook if danger is involved.

If a man prepares dinner for you and the salad contains three or more types of lettuce, he is serious.

Men who can eat anything and not gain weight should do so out of sight of women.

Not one man in any beer advert has a beer belly.

Why do married men gain weight while bachelors don't?
Bachelors go to the refrigerator, see nothing they want, then
go to bed. Married guys go to bed, see nothing they want,
then go to the fridge.

Men only think about candlelit dinners if the power goes
off.

It takes three men to make popcorn: one to hold the pan and
the other two to act macho and shake the stove.

Beer bellies exist because the rib that God removed from
Adam to make Eve was the one supposed to hold in his
stomach.

Men and Sport

When four or more women get together, they talk about men.
When four or more men get together, they talk about sports.

If you want attention from a man, don't get involved with him during the play-off season of any sport.

The owners of most sports teams are men, which may explain why every year the cheerleaders' outfits get tighter while the players' get baggier.

Men forget everything – that's why they need instant replays in sports.

The difference between a golf ball and a woman's G-spot is that a man will spend twenty minutes looking for the golf ball.

A man who asks his wife if she's lost weight has just spent their last £100 on a new fly-fishing rod.

If a man suggests you take a break from vacuuming the living room and relax, it's because he can't hear the football on the telly.

If football is a man's game, it's generally because women are too smart to play it.

13 Things You'll Never Hear a Man Say . . .

While I'm up, can I get anything for you?

No, I don't want another beer. I have to work tomorrow.

Sometimes I just want to be held.

I think we're lost. Let's pull over and ask for directions

I'm really ill, but fear not – I can fend for myself.

Her tits are just too big.

We haven't been shopping for ages – let's go look at some new carpets.

Damn these onions, pass me a hanky.

I think Barry Manilow's a groovin' sex machine.

No, I insist – you made the bed last week. It's my turn.

This movie has too much nudity.

Forget Match of the Day – let's watch Gardener's World.

I understand . . .

Why Beer is Better Than Women (So They Say)

You don't have to wine and dine a beer.

Your beer will always wait patiently for you in the car.

A beer doesn't get jealous when you grab another beer.

When you go to a pub, you know you can always pick up another beer.

You can have a beer in public.

A frigid beer is a good beer.

Beer looks the same in the morning.

Beer doesn't have a mother.

Beer doesn't go crazy once a month.

Beer doesn't whine, it bubbles.

Beer is never overweight.

If you change beers, you don't have to pay alimony.

Beer doesn't mind the football season.

A beer is always ready to leave on time.

A beer doesn't want you to hold it after you've finished.

50 Reasons to be a Man

Phone conversations are over in 30 seconds maximum.

A five-day holiday requires only one suitcase.

You know stuff about tanks.

You can open all your own jars.

Old friends don't care if you've lost or gained weight.

At clubs, the queues for the men's are 80 per cent shorter.

Your bum isn't a factor in job interviews.

All your orgasms are real.

You can leave the hotel bed unmade.

You can kill your own food.

The garage is all yours.

You get extra credit for the slightest act of thoughtfulness.

You never have to clean a toilet.

You can be showered and ready to go in ten minutes.

Sex means never having to worry about your reputation.

Wedding plans take care of themselves.

If someone forgets to invite you to something, he or she can still be your friend.

Your underwear is £10 for a three-pack.

You don't have to shave below your neck.

If you're 34 and single, no one even notices.

You can write your name in the snow.

Chocolate is just another snack.

Three pairs of shoes is more than enough.

You get to think about sex 90 per cent of your waking hours.

Foreplay is optional.

Nobody stops telling a good dirty joke when you walk into the room.

You can whip your shirt off on a hot day.

You don't have to clear your house if the meter reader's coming by.

Car mechanics tell you the truth.

You don't care if no one notices your new haircut.

You never feel compelled to stop a pal from getting laid.

You know at least 20 ways to open a beer bottle.

You can sit with your knees apart no matter what you're wearing.

One mood, all the time!

Gray hair and wrinkles only add character.

Wedding dress: £2,000; tuxedo rental: £75.

If you retain water, it's in a canteen.

The remote control is yours and yours alone.

People don't glance at your chest when you're talking to them.

You can drop by to see a friend without bringing a little gift.

You have a normal and healthy relationship with your mother.

You can buy condoms without the shopkeeper imagining you naked.

You needn't pretend you're "freshening up" to go to the bathroom.

If you don't call your pal when you say you will, he won't tell your other friends you've changed.

The occasional well-rendered belch is practically expected.

If something mechanical doesn't work, you can bash it with a hammer or throw it across the room.

You don't have to remember everyone's birthdays and anniversaries.

Not liking a person doesn't preclude having great sex with them.

Your pals can be trusted never to trap you with: "So . . . notice anything different?"

Porn movies are designed with your mind in mind.

There's always a game on somewhere.

10 Reasons Not to be a Man

You have to take out the garbage.

The Ferrari 550 Maranello is listed at over £200,000.

No sofas in men's toilets.

External genitalia are vulnerable to knees and footballs.

Even if you get your head caught in an industrial woodchipper, you're not allowed to cry.

James Bond movies only come out once every two years.

Ribbed for her pleasure, not for yours.

You have to wear ties.

You can't flirt your way out of a jam.

"Women and children first!"

Reasons Why It's Great to be a Woman

Sometimes it seems men have it all their own way – so here's a quick reminder of all the advantages of being a woman.

You never have to buy your own drinks.

You can get out of speeding tickets by crying.

You're not expected to know how cars work.

You can sleep your way to the top.

You don't worry about losing your hair.

You always get to choose the movie.

You don't have to mow the lawn.

You don't have to understand the offside rule.

You can marry rich and not have to work.

You never have to use a power drill.

You never run out of excuses.

You get expensive jewellery as gifts that you never have to give back.

You get gifts all the time because men mess up so often.

You can give 'the look' that makes men cower in the corner.

You can dance.

You look good in shorts.

You have mastered civilized eating.

You are better gossips.

You look better naked than men.

Women do less time for violent crime.

You can wear no underwear and be considered wild and sexy; a man who does the same thing is merely thought of as disgusting.

Short women are petite; short men are just short.

You don't need an excuse to be in a bad mood.

CHAPTER 2

What Men
Are Like . . .

Sometimes it's easier to understand something if you compare it with something else. This is particularly useful when trying to understand men, whose habits, behaviour and outlook on life seem so often completely incomprehensible from a woman's point of view. A glance at the following list should give you some unexpected insights into the male psyche.

Men are like Animals – Messy and potentially violent . . . But they make great pets.

Men are like Babies – They are cute at first . . . But you soon get tired of cleaning up after them.

Men are like Bananas – The older they get the less firm they are.

Men are like Bank Accounts – Without a lot of money they don't generate much interest.

Men are like Baseball Bats – The quality of being long and hard doesn't always guarantee a score.

Men are like Blenders – You know you need one . . . But you are not quite sure why.

Men are like Bricks and Mortar – After getting laid they take a long time to get hard.

Men are like Bunions – The only relief you can get is when you are off your feet.

Men are like Buttons – They are always popping off at the wrong time.

Men are like Caterpillars – They got where they are by a lot of crawling.

Men are like Character Actors – When they show any character, they are acting.

Men are like Chocolate Bars – Smooth, and they usually head right for your hips.

Men are like Cliffs – Most are just a big bluff.

Men are like Clocks – Their hands are always moving over figures.

Men are like Coffee – The best types are rich and warm, and can keep you going all night long.

Men are like Colds – You can never get rid of the bad ones in a hurry.

Men are like Commercials – You cannot believe a word they say.

Men are like Computers – Hard to figure out and never have enough memory.

Men are like Cookies – Underneath, most are just plain crumbs.

Men are like Coolers – Load them up with beer and you can take them anywhere.

Men are like Copiers – You need them for reproduction . . . But that's about it.

Men are like Crowbars – They are not much to crow about, and some are better behind bars.

Men are like Crystal – Some look good, but you can still see through them.

Men are like Curling Irons – They are always hot . . . And they are always in your hair.

Men are like Dawn – Full of promise . . . But usually turns out to be the same old routine.

Men are like Department Stores – Their clothes always seem to be half off.

Men are like Diamonds – In their natural state, they are rough and ugly . . . If you want them polished, you have to do it yourself.

Men are like Drips – You can hear them, but you can't turn them off.

Men are like Dry Cleaners – Most work fast and leave no ring.

Men are like Elephants – Because they are bigger, they think they are "King of the Jungle".

Men are like Firemen – No matter what they are doing, they can be ready to respond in minutes.

Men are like Fish – They keep getting into trouble when they can't keep their mouths shut.

Men are like Flowers – They are often potted.

Men are like Forests – It takes an expert to spot the rotten ones.

Men are like Goats – They just love to butt in.

Men are like Government Bonds – Usually a sure thing, but they take too long to mature.

Men are like Horoscopes – They always tell you what to do, and usually they are wrong.

Men are like Instant Coffee – Easy to make.

Men are like Lava Lamps – Fun to watch sometimes . . . But not all that bright.

Men are like Lawn Mowers – If you are not pushing one around, then you are riding it.

Men are like Lightning – Known for its occasional flashes of bright light, but not much else.

Men are like Magicians – They can turn almost anything into an argument.

Men are like Mascara – Difficult to handle . . . And runs at the first sign of emotion.

Men are like Mini Skirts – If you are not careful, they will creep up your legs.

Men are like Noodles – They are always in hot water, they lack taste, and they need dough.

Men are like Palaces – Stunning ones exist, but only in fairy tales.

Men are like Parking Spaces – They are all taken.

Men are like Pigs – They don't usually contract mad cow disease.

Men are like Pillows – A real pleasure at first . . . But eventually, even the best ones become soft and lumpy.

Men are like Place Mats – They show up . . . But only when there is food on the table.

Men are like Plants – Some will only flourish if you keep them in the dark.

Men are like Plastic Wrap – Cheap and clingy . . . And very easy to see through.

Men are like Plungers – They spend most of their lives in a hardware store or the bathroom.

Men are like Popcorn – They satisfy you, but only for a little while.

Men are like Potato Chips – You know they are bad for you . . . But one is never enough.

Men are like Power Tools – They make a lot of noise . . . And you can never find them when you need them.

Men are like Remote Controls – Simple and easy to use . . . And usually located lying around the TV.

Men are like Restaurants – You have to wait a half-hour or more for service.

Men are like Rivers – The largest part is their mouths.

Men are like Road Kill – They lie around . . . Until they begin to smell.

Men are like Scales – They give you the answer you didn't want.

Men are like Shag Carpets – Soft and fuzzy . . . And extremely easy to walk on.

Men are like Snowstorms – You never know how many inches you will get, or how long it will last.

Men are like Soap Operas – They are fun to watch . . . But don't believe everything you hear.

Men are like Spray paint – One squeeze and they are all over you.

Men are like Theories – They hardly ever work.

Men are like Thunderstorms – You never know when they are coming.

Men are like Ties – Expensive . . . And serve no practical purpose.

Men are like Tiles – Lay them right and you can walk on them for years.

Men are like Tyres – Full of hot air . . . And bald as they age.

Men are like Trucks – Most of the time, they have a load on.

Men are like TVs – You can turn them on instantly.

Men are like Umbrellas – Once you learn how to manage them, they are easy to open up.

Men are like Used Cars – Lots available . . . But cheap and unreliable.

Men are like Vacations – They never seem to be long enough.

Men are like Vacuum Cleaners – They are not much fun . . . But at least you can push them around.

Men are like the Weather – Nothing at all can be done to make it change.

Men are like Wheelbarrows – They need pushing, and are liable to fall over when you let go.

Men are like Wind – Generate a lot of air, which can be either hot or cold.

Men are like Wine – Made by stamping on the raw material and keeping it in the dark until maturity.

CHAPTER 3

A Guide to Chat-up Lines

The chat-up line is the first move a man or woman makes in the dating game. Women, naturally, have the edge on men when it comes to style and flair, while men's contributions can range from the arrogant to the idiotic, with only a few experts able to kindle that spark with a few, well-chosen words. Here's a useful guide to help you decide your next move.

A Good Bet

If I could rearrange the alphabet I would put U and I together.

Your father must have been a thief because he stole all the stars from the night sky and put them in your eyes.

When you fell from heaven, did it hurt?

I have a heart condition. It seems to get broken a lot. You wouldn't happen to have a cure for me would you?

Someone better call the police, 'cause it's got to be illegal to be that good-looking!

Girl, you must be a parking ticket because you got "fine" written all over you.

What time is it? Well, we've got to hurry, we've only got a few more minutes to be the fastest couple to fall in love in history!

If you were a new hamburger at McDonalds, they'd call you McGorgeous.

I brought you this rose so the rose would know what real beauty is.

If you were blue and I was yellow, my favourite colour would be green.

I didn't know angels flew so low.

If I had the power to create the perfect woman, I'd leave you just the way you are.

You must be Jamaican, cause you're Jamaican me crazy.

If you held 11 roses in front of a mirror you would see 12 of the most beautiful things in the world.

I know that milk does a body good, but how much damn milk have you been drinking?

If you were a tear in my eye, I wouldn't cry for fear of losing you.

Excuse me, but could you give me directions? To where? Your heart . . .

You know you might be asked to leave soon, you're making the other women look bad.

Excuse me, Miss, I believe you dropped something... my jaw.

Is your personality as pretty as your eyes?

Can I have my heart back now, please..

If I was to die tonight, I would die happy, because I have met someone as beautiful as you!

Baby, somebody better call God, cuz he's missing an angel!

God must have cried when you left heaven!

You're so sweet, you're gonna put sugar out of business.

I found this rose and figured it had to belong to someone as beautiful as you.

Somebody call the cops 'cause it's got to be illegal to look that good.

Now I understand why the sky has been grey all day! Why? Because all the blue is in your eyes!

Life without you is like a broken pencil. Pointless.

I bet you're tired of hearing pickup lines, when words can't compare or express the true nature of your beauty!

You know what they say about beauty... it protects against all evil. Well, with you I feel really safe!

Can you catch? I think I'm falling for you.

If water were beauty, you'd be an ocean.

Can I flirt with you?

Have you seen [any movie]? Would you like to?

Careful! (Probably Dodgy)

All those curves, and me with no brakes.

I lost my teddy bear, so will you sleep with me tonight?

Just call me milk 'cause I'll do your body good.

If I follow you home, will you keep me?

I wish I had a swing like that in my backyard.

Are you Greek? Because I thought all goddesses were from Greece.

You look too good to be alone.

If looks were money, you'd be rich.

I'm new in town. Can you give me directions to your flat?

Do you have a map? I just keep getting lost in your eyes!

Excuse me, but I can't help but notice how much you have been noticing me noticing you!

Are we dead? Why? Because I thought angels only lived in heaven.

Have you entered a beauty contest and they have said, "Sorry, no professionals"?

If I were yours, and you were mine, I wouldn't be asking you for your name.

Is that your perfume or the smell of passion?

Hey, baby, you're so hot I had to turn off my smoke alarm.

I would crawl naked in the cold rain, on broken glass, just to hear you speak over the telephone!

Here, you look a bit tired, let me breathe for you!

Point to the sky and say, "Excuse me, but heaven is that way!"

Is there a rainbow, because you're the treasure I've been searching for.

I don't love you, but I could!

Hello, I'm a thief, and I'm here to steal your heart.

(With hands on shoulders) Oh, those are shoulder blades, I
thought they were wings.

Do you have a twin sister? Do they call her Barbie?
It's women like you who stop me from becoming a monk

Your dad must have been a king for a day to have a
princess like you!

Wow, you're not just beautiful, but you're clever as
well . . .

Is there an airport nearby or is that just my heart taking off?

You know, you look really hot! You must be the real reason for global warming.

If I could be one thing in the world, I'd be a tear born in your eye, living on your cheek and dying on your lips.

If a kiss was a snow flake, I would send you a whole blizzard .

Excuse me, but do you have a life jacket? Why? Because I'm drowning in your eyes!

You remind me of a compass because I'd be lost without you.

If you left now, you'd just being running away with my heart.

I didn't believe in angels until I met you!

What can I do to make you mine?

You're what God was thinking of when He said, "Let there be woman."

I saw your picture in the dictionary today… next to the word "beautiful".

Your lips are like wine and I want to get drunk.

I have had a really bad day and it always makes me feel better to see a pretty girl smile. So, would you smile for me?

So there you are! I've been looking all over for you, the girl of my dreams!

Save me, I'm drowning in a sea of love!

Do your legs hurt from running through my dreams all night?

Nice to meet you, I'm [your name] and you are . . . gorgeous!

Your name is Sandra, huh? Can I call you Sandy? Really, what time?

Hi, my name's [xxx], how do you like me so far?

Do you have a library card? Good, 'cause I wanna check you out!

Your warm eyes melt the iciness of my heart.

Have you always been this cute, or did you have to work at it?

Hi. I suffer from amnesia. Do I come here often?

He: (as she's leaving) Hey, aren't you forgetting
something?
She: What?
He: Me!

Pardon me, what pickup line works best with you?

I think I can die happy now, 'cause I've just seen a piece of
heaven.

I'd spend money on you I haven't even made.

As the sun illuminates the moon and the stars, so let us
illuminate each other.

Are you going places or just being taken?

Baby, if you were a flower, I would pick you!

I'm not drunk, I'm just intoxicated by you.

I can't decide if you are a better person than you are a woman or you are a better woman than you are a person.

Baby, you must be a broom, cause you just swept me off my feet.

Baby, you're so fine, you're my 9.9 . . .

Hey, didn't we go to different schools together?

Would you like gin and platonic, or would you prefer scotch and sofa?

I have only three months to live . . .

Do you have a boyfriend? Well, when you want a MANfriend, come and talk to me.

I was sitting here holding this cigarette and I realized I'd rather be holding you.

You are as beautiful as the Venus de Milo… except you have arms.

Run a Mile

Baby, I'm not Fred Flintstone, but I could make your Bedrock.

You know, I might not be the best looking guy in here . . . But I'm the only one who's talking to you.

Hey, baby, why don't we go behind a rock and get a little boulder?

I lost my phone number. Can I have yours?

Baby, are those moon pants you're wearing? 'Cause your ass is out of this world!

Hi, I'm a gynaecologist and I give free exams.

Hey, you wouldn't happen to have a socket for my pocket rocket, would you?

I sure like what you're wearing . . . can I talk you out of it?

If you were a plumber, you could empty my pipes all day!

If you were a bank, I would make a deposit and then withdraw.

You're too smooth. I think you need a hump!

I'll take a piece of anything that you will give me.

How many women do I have to kill to get your attention?

Excuse me, I'm a bird watcher and I'm looking for a big-breasted bed thrasher. Have you seen one?

If you're going to regret this in the morning, then we can sleep until the afternoon.

Hi, I'm a necrophiliac. How good are you at playing dead?

Are those erasers in your bra or are you just happy to see me?

Excuse me, I was just admiring your lung capacity.

I'm looking for a lovely, successful business woman whose hobby is housework.

I'd marry you tomorrow if we could have the honeymoon tonight.

Is it hot in here, or is it just you?

Do you want to come see my hard drive? I promise it isn't 3.5 inches and it ain't floppy.

If you've lost your virginity, can I have the box it came in?

That's a nice smile you've got, it's a shame it's not all you're wearing!

I lost my virginity . . . Can I have yours?

Do I know you from somewhere, because I don't recognise you with your clothes on!

What do you like for breakfast?

You look a lot like my third wife . . . of course, I've only been married twice!

If I told you that you remind me of my mum, would you tuck me into bed tonight?

I play the field, and it looks like I just hit a home run with you.

Whatever you do, don't ever cut that silky hair of yours!

I think that you are the most beautiful girl I've ever seen . . . on a Wednesday!

Let's go to my place and do the things I'll tell everyone we did anyway.

[Grab her tush.] Pardon me, is this seat taken?

So . . . How am I doin'?

[Tap your thigh] You just think this is my leg.

Excuse me, you don't know me but I think you should.

You have been a very naughty girl! Now go to my room!

Do you have any Italian in you? Would you like some?

Hi, the voices in my head told me to come talk to you!

Hey baby, you want to see something swell?

Are you religious? 'Cause I'm the answer to all your prayers!

You know, I never was too good at maths . . . like, if, I put you and me together, I'd get 69.

You know the more I drink, the prettier you get!

Was your father a farmer? Because you sure have grown some nice melons!

Bond. James Bond.

You look like the type of girl who has heard every line in the book. So, what's one more?

Her: What do you think of this (dress, sweater, blouse, etc.)?
Him: I like nothing better.

Walk up to a lady at a social gathering (party, club, etc.) and simply ask, "Are you ready to go home now?"

At the dinner table, if you eat together, pick up the bread and ask, "Wanna roll?"

You know, you've got the prettiest teeth I've ever dreamed of coming across.

Think you can dance in those shoes?

OK, you can stand next to me as long as you don't talk about the heat.

You're "No Parking", right? Just trying to guess your sign.

Why don't you surprise your room-mate/parents and not go home tonight?

Good looking waitress pouring a drink: Say when!
Guy: As soon as I finish this drink.

If I weren't so romantic, I'd shoot you.

My lenses turn dark in the sunshine of your love.

I know a great way to burn off the calories from that pastry you just ate.

Was your father a mechanic? Then how did you get such a finely tuned body?

Baby, you look better and better each day . . . and tonight, you look like tomorrow!

She: Gee, I really enjoyed myself tonight!
He: Me, too. Maybe we could let our bodies enjoy each other sometime!

You know, I would die happy if I saw you naked just once!

Excuse me, do you live around here often?

I've gotta thirst, baby, and you smell like my Gatorade!

I'm on fire, baby, can I run through your sprinkler?

Hi! I'm Big Brother, and I've been watching you!

Where have you been all my life?

Don't worry about it. Nothing that you've ever done before counts. The only thing that matters is that we're together.

Hey, don't I know you? Yeah, you're the girl with the beautiful smile

Want to see my stamp collection?

Hey, baby, do you believe in love at first sight, or do I have to walk past you a second time?

Baby, I'm an American Express lover . . . you shouldn't go home without me!

You: I'm sorry, were you talking to me?
Her: No.
You: Well then, please start.

Can I see your tan lines?

If your parents hadn't met I'd be a very unhappy man right now!

You see my friend over there? [Point to friend who sheepishly waves from afar.] He wants to know if YOU think I'M cute.

Hey, baby, you must be a light switch, 'cause every time I see you, you turn me on!

Stand still so I can pick you up!

Hi, we're taking a survey and I need your phone number. If you give it to me, I'll call you and tell you the results.

Do you like music? (Yes) Good, I've got a great stereo in my car!

Are you looking for Mr. Right or Mr. Right Now?

You make my software turn to hardware!

I'll show you mine if you'll show me yours.
Girl, you've got more curves than a back-country road!

How to Get Rid of Him

Man: "Haven't I seen you somewhere before?"
Woman: "Yeah, that's why I don't go there anymore."

Man: "Is this seat empty?"
Woman: "Yeah, and this one will be, too, if you sit down."

Man: "So, wanna go back to my place?"
Woman: "Well, I don't know. Will two people fit under a rock?"

Man: "So, what do you do for a living?"
Woman: "I'm a female impersonator."

Man: "Hey, come on, we're both here at this bar for the same reason."
Woman: "Yeah! Let's pick up some birds!"

Man: "I know how to please a woman."
Woman: "Then please leave me alone."

Man: "I want to give myself to you."
Woman: "Sorry, I don't accept cheap gifts."

Man: "I would go to the end of the world for you."
Woman: "Yes, but would you stay there?"

You know, I'd really love to screw your brains out, but it appears someone has already beaten me to it.

Man : "Haven't we met before?"
Woman: "Yes, I'm the receptionist at the STD clinic."

Man: "Your place or mine?"
Woman: "Both. You go to yours and I'll go to mine."

Man: "I'd like to call you. What's your number?"
Woman: "It's in the phone book."
Man: "But I don't know your name."
Woman: "That's in the phone book, too."

Man: "Hey, baby, what's your sign?"
Woman: "Do Not Enter."

Man: "How do you like your eggs in the morning?"
Woman: "Unfertilised!"

Man: "If I could see you naked, I'd die happy."
Woman: "Yeah, but if I saw you naked, I'd probably die laughing."

Man: "Your body is like a temple."
Woman: "Sorry, there are no services today."

Man: "I'd go through anything for you."
Woman: "Good! Let's start with your bank account."

Try Some Yourself

Your lips are like wine and I want to get drunk.

Did you know we are all naked under our clothes?

You've got the ship, I've got the harbour . . . let's say we tie up for the night?

Hey, baby, I'm a missionary and I'm looking for a position.

Is your father a baker? Because you've got great buns!

I forgot your name, can I just call you mine?

Was your father an alien? Because there's nothing else like you on earth!

You are the reason women fall in love.

What time do you have to be back in heaven?

If you walk away now, I'll die with a broken heart.

Are you a dead ringer for a Greek god or what?

Quick! call 999, you just stole my heart!

When I look into your eyes I see the moon and the stars.

You know, you look a lot like my next boyfriend.

[Look at his shirt label. When he asks, "What are you doing?"] Checking to see if you were made in heaven.

Were you a Boy Scout because you sure have tied my heart in a knot.

I can sense that you're a terrific lover, and it intimidates me a little.

So, what are the chances that we can engage in anything more than just conversation?

(At the photocopier) Reproducing, eh? Mind if I help?

My dad said never talk to a stranger, so can I have your name?

Can I flirt with you?

CHAPTER 4

The Rules

Men may have established and controlled the rules of the Relationship Game in the past but that's all changed now: women get to play on an equal footing. So here are the *New Rules* in a specially simplified version so that every man can read, understand and follow with minimum effort – plus a reminder of the *Old Rules*, now superseded, and a handy checklist of *Things a Man Shouldn't Say to a Woman when Making Love*.

The New Rules: 50 Rules Designed by Women for Men (or "The Proper Way for Men to Behave Towards Women")

1. Call.

2. Never lie.

3. The correct answer to, "Do I look fat?" is never "Yes".

4. Ditto for, "Is she prettier than me?"

5. Ordering for her is good. Telling her what she wants is bad.

6. Being attentive is good. Stalking is bad.

7. "Honey", "Darling" and "Sweetheart" are good. "Nag", "Lardass" and "Bitch" are bad.

8. Talking is good. Shouting is bad. Slapping is a major crime.

9. A grunt is not an acceptable answer to a question.

10. None of your ex-girlfriends were ever nicer, prettier or better in bed.

11. Her cooking is excellent – so tell her.

12. But this isn't an excuse to avoid cooking for her.

13. Soap is your friend.

14. Wearing no hat in the rain does not equal shower; aftershave does not equal soap; and warm does not equal clean.

15. Buying her dinner does not equal foreplay.

16. Answering, "Who was that on the phone?" with, "Nobody", is never going to end that conversation.

17. Ditto for, "Whose lipstick is this?"

18. Two words – clean socks.

19. Believe it or not, you are probably not more attractive when you are drunk.

20. Burping is not sexy.

21. You are always wrong!

22. You are sorry!

23. She is probably less impressed by your discourse on your cool car than you think she is.

24. Ditto for your discourse on football.

25. Ditto for your ability to jump up and hit any awning in a single bound.

26. If a boys' night out is going to be fun, invite the girls.

27. If a boys' night out is going to involve strippers, remember the rules at the zoo: "No petting".

28. "Will you marry me?" is good. "Let's shack up together", is bad.

29. Don't assume PMS is the cause for every bad mood.

30. Don't assume PMS doesn't exist.

31. "No" means no. "Yes" means yes. Silence could mean anything. Any of these could mean the opposite, depending on circumstance. Practise reading her mind.

32. "But we kiss . . ." is not justification for using her toothbrush. You don't clean plaque with your tongue.

33. Never let her walk anywhere alone after 11 p.m.

34. Chivalry and feminism are not mutually exclusive.

35. Pick her up at the airport – don't whine – just do it.

36. If you want to break up with her – break up with her.
Don't act like a complete idiot until she does it for you.

37. Don't tell her you love her if you don't.

38. Tell her you love her if you do – often.

39. Always suck up to her brother.

40. Think boxers: silk boxers.

41. Don't move all her bottles off the bathroom shelf: they are there for a reason.

42. Remember Valentine's Day.

43. Remember <u>all</u> anniversaries, including the day you met.

44. Don't try to change the way she dresses.

45. Her haircut is never bad.

46. Don't let your friends pick on her.

47. Send a post-card when you go away, preferably not with a naked girl on the front.

48. Buy her flowers, and not only when you've done something wrong.

49. Never spend Saturday afternoon watching football when you could be spending a day with her at the seaside.

50. Try to be intelligent, even if it takes effort and evening classes.

The Old Rules: 50 Rules Designed By Men For Men (or "The Wrong Way for Men to Behave Towards Women")

1. Don't call her, ever.

2. If you don't like a girl, don't tell her. It's more fun to let her figure it out by herself.

3. Lie.

4. Always be as ambiguous as possible. If you don't want to answer (or cannot), a grunt or two will do.

5. Always remember that you're a man, therefore, no matter what happens in a relationship, it isn't your fault.

6. Never ask for help. Even if you really need help – don't ask. Other men will think you're a wimp.

7. Remember that women seem to like it when you totally ignore them. It arouses them.

8. If you have to talk to a girl on the phone for more than three minutes, use only monosyllabic words and noises. Bodily noises are permissible.

9. One sure way to make a girl like you is to go after her best friend. She will then see what she's missing.

10. Tell her you will call. Then, refer back to rule number 1.

11. Don't wear matching clothes. People will think your girlfriend picked them out, and it will cramp your style.

12. A good break-up line is: "It's not you, it's me."

13. Don't have a clue. However, if you should get a clue, pretend you didn't and disregard it.

14. Remember that if you don't get sex whenever you want, your equipment will suffer.

15. If any other male asks, you have had sex in all possible positions and locations. Improvise if necessary.

16. Life is one big competition. If someone is better than you at anything, pretend it's not true, or pretend it's unimportant.

17. Do not make decisions about relationships. If you are backed into a corner, then stall. If you still must decide, always leave a large loophole for your escape.

18. Remember that almost every sentence that anyone says has a phrase or two that can be contorted to have sexual meaning.

19. As a general rule, if whatever you're doing does not satisfy you completely in 5–10 minutes, it's really not worth the bother.

20. It's permissible to apologize as long as you don't mean it.

21. The same with hurting someone, you can pretend you care or that you regret something, as long as you really don't.

22. Try to have a good memory, but if you forget certain things, for example her birthday, her eye colour or the names of your kids, it's not the end of the world.

23. Ignorance solves certain problems. What you don't know can't hurt you.

24. It is never your duty to take responsibility for your actions.

25. Girls don't care what you do to them as long as they get to please you.

26. Don't ever notice anything.

27. If you are dating someone but love someone else, don't say anything. Wait until the girl you are dating falls in love with you, and then tell her.

28. Basic fundamental rule of dating: quantity, not quality.

29. Basic fundamental rule of sex: quantity is quality.

30. If you cheat on a girl, but no one finds out, then technically you've done nothing wrong.

31. Crying is not manly. Then again, if you are a real man, what the hell do you have to cry about anyway?

32. If the question begins with "why", it is better to answer "I don't know", because most of these questions are a trap.

33. Remember that every virgin girl could be saving herself for a guy just like you.

34. If you ever find yourself in a position where you have been proved wrong, blame others. Come up with creative and believable reasons why they are at fault and not you.

35. Keep track of how often you think about sex daily. Compare with other men.

36. If you're on a date, and there is a lull in the conversation, tell the girl how many different women you have had sex with during the past hour/day/week/month.

37. Practise your blank stare.

38. If you are ever forced to show emotion, just pick random emotions like rage, lust and insanity, and display them at random, inconvenient times. You won't be asked to do it again.

39. If you are asked to do something by your girlfriend or wife that you don't want to do, first try your manly best to get out of it. If that doesn't work, go ahead and do what you were asked to do, but complain that you don't know how to do it and continuously ask questions on how to do each part. If she doesn't rush in to do it for you, finish the job in a half-hearted fashion so she will never ask you to do it again.

40. Work out day and night to make your body even more beautiful than it already is. When a girl asks you if you've been working out, say things like, "No, Baby, I was born like this".

41. Drink beer, then more beer.

42. Take your girlfriend out with your mates, then ignore her completely.

43. Tell jokes that embarrass her so she goes home alone. Then you can begin to talk seriously.

44. Always leave the toilet seat in the up position.

45. Never send your girlfriend a Valentine card, or if you do, say that it's one you received last year and you are saving the world's forests by recycling.

46. Watch football frequently, especially when she wants to watch wildlife programmes.

47. Invite your mates round when she's engrossed in a cliff-hanger episode of her favourite soap.

48. Never clean the bath, in fact never clean anything, unless you want the job for life.

49. When she crashes the car, make her feel really bad about it so she never wants to drive again.

50. Don't let her drive in the first place is a better rule: a man in the passenger seat doesn't look up to much, especially at traffic lights.

Things a Man Shouldn't Say to a Woman When Making Love

You look just like your mother.

Did you remember to lock the back door?

And to think, I was really trying to pick up your friend!

You carry on, but do you mind if I finish this book?

What's for dinner tomorrow?

It's my mobile! I must answer it.

I can see right up your nose.

Oh, by the way, the cat got run over this afternoon.

That boil on your chin looks nasty.

Did I tell you my Aunt Winifred died in this bed?

Linda used to do that.

Do you accept Visa?

Did I mention the video camera?

Hurry up – this room rents by the hour.

Sorry about that – must be the baked beans.

This would be fun with a few more people.

I've just thought of the answer to 3 down. I won't be a second.

I see that mad axeman's still on the loose.

Is that it? Can I go now?

CHAPTER 5

Understanding What He Says

What He Says and What He Means

Men's verbal skills, being much more primitive than those of women, demand some decoding in order to get at the real meaning. Here's a handy guide to help you get at the truth.

What he says:
Let's get married.
What he means:
Let's get married for a while.

What he says:
Let's get married right away.
What he means:
I'm broke.

What he says:
Of course I'll always love you.
What he means:
I want to watch this.

What he says:
Would you like another drink?
What he means:
Another one of those and you're mine.

What he says:
I think I'll get another drink.
What he means:
Buy me a drink.

What he says:
I'm hungry.
What he means:
Make me some dinner.

What he says:
I'm really hungry.
What he means:
Make me some dinner now.

What he says:
Have you seen my shirt?
What he means:
Have you washed my shirt?

What he says:
Did you enjoy that?
What he means:
Tell me I'm the best ever.

What he says:
Yes, I love your new hairstyle.
What he means:
What new hairstyle?

What he says:
She's got nice hair.
What he means:
Cut your hair like that.

What he says:
She's wearing a nice skirt.
What he means:
Buy a skirt like that.

What he says:
Last night was great.
What he means:
Who are you again?

What he says:
I was thinking about last night.
What he means:
You looked a lot cuter when I was drunk.

What he says:
I'm an old fashioned romantic.
What he means:
I'm broke.

What he says:
I think we should just be friends.
What he means:
Bye!

What he says:
Let's spend Christmas with your folks.
What he means:
Your sister is cute.

What he says:
I think women should be valued as people.
What he means:
Those are great breasts.

What he says:
I've learned a lot from our relationship.
What he means:
I think your best friend is cute.

What he says:
I need you back.
What he means:
Nobody else will sleep with me.

What he says:
She's not my type.
What he means:
She said no.

What he says:
I know exactly where we are.
What he means:
What country is this again?

What he says:
The remote needs new batteries.
What he means:
Get up and change the channel.

What he says:
You expect too much from me.
What he means:
I have to sleep after sex.

What he says:
I've moved on.
What he means:
She got a restraining order.

What he says:
She didn't fulfil my needs.
What he means:
She dumped me.

What he says:
It was complicated.
What he means:
I have no idea what happened.

What he says:
I'm totally over it.
What he means:
I cry myself to sleep.

What he says:
Would you like to get some coffee?
What he means:
Let's have sex at some point in the future.

What he says:
I've got tickets to a great movie.
What he means:
Let's have sex quite soon.

What he says:
I'll take you to dinner.
What he means:
Let's have sex tonight.

What he says:
I'm not ready to commit.
What he means:
Nobody will go out with me more than once.

What he says:
How old do I look?
What he means:
A cute girl called me "sir".

What he says:
I do help around the house.
What he means:
I washed up in 1996.

What he says:
You look good today.
What he means:
I'm going to ask for something big.

What he says:
Have you lost weight?
What he means:
I'm going to ask for something really big.

What he says:
What do you mean you have nothing to wear?
What he means:
I swear you went shopping for clothes three years ago.

What he says:
That one looks great on you.
What he means:
Please God, let's go home.

What he says:
Can I help with dinner?
What he means:
Why isn't it ready yet?

What he says:
I got a lot done while you were away
What he means:
I caught up on all the soaps

What he says:
I'm getting a lot more exercise these days.
What he means:
I lost the TV remote.

What he says:
That's a woman's job.
What he means:
That sounds hard and boring.

What he says:
I'll fix it later
What he means:
Maybe you'll get fed up and buy a new one.

What he says:
I have my reasons.
What he means:
I didn't even think about it.

What he says:
You're working too hard.
What he means:
Turn off the vacuum, I can't hear the TV

What he says:
I agree.
What he means:
What did she say?

What he says:
I've just got things on my mind
What he means:
I can't work out if you're wearing a bra or not.

What he says:
I am listening.
What he means:
Look at the legs on that blonde.

What he says:
That's an interesting point of view.
What he means:
I wasn't listening to a word you said.

What he says:
I saw this flower stall and thought of you.
What he means:
The flower seller was a babe.

What he says:
Of course I'm not lost.
What he means:
We are a thousand miles from civilization.

What he says:
It's the thought that counts.
What he means:
The gas station was the only place open when I
remembered it was our anniversary.

What he says:
I'm going fishing with the guys.
What he means:
I'm going to sit near water and drink a lot.

What he says:
It's a guy thing.
What he means:
There is absolutely no rational explanation.

What he says:
It's too difficult to explain.
What he means:
I have no idea why.

What he says:
Good idea.
What he means:
That will never work.

What he says:
It's a classic movie.
What he means:
There are fast cars, naked babes and firearms.

What he says:
I can't find my keys, trousers, shoes . . .
What he means:
They aren't painted luminous orange with a flashing light
on top.

What he says:
I missed you.
What he means:
Where the hell did you hide the food and my clean clothes?

What he says:
She's one of those feminists.
What he means:
She's not into sport.

What he says:
I think she's a lesbian.
What he means:
She is into sport.

What he says:
What's wrong?
What he means:
No sex tonight then?

What he says:
Let me give you a massage.
What he means:
Let me get your clothes off.

What he says:
I have something to tell you.
What he means:
You're going to regret you ever met me.

What he says:
My boss is unreasonable.
What he means:
He expects me to go to work.

What he says:
That new look is great.
What he means:
My God, what have you done?

What he says:
This tastes great.
What he means:
I must buy a smoke alarm tomorrow.

What he says:
Paint it any colour you like.
What he means:
Paint it white or I'll complain for years.

What he says:
Woman driver!
What he means:
She's under the speed limit.

What he says:
I left plenty of gas in your car.
What he means:
I advise you to start downhill.

What he says:
I brought you a present.
What he means:
It was a give-away.

What he says:
I'm going hunting with the guys.
What he means:
I'm going to sit near trees and drink a lot.

What he says:
I'll call you tomorrow.
What he means:
I don't have your phone number.

What he says:
Of course I want to see you again.
What he means:
I'm leaving town tomorrow.

What he says:
I've seen the classics.
What he means:
I accidentally saw a black and white movie once.

What he says:
It's only a little cut.
What he means:
It's agony but I won't admit it.

What he says:
I think I'm going to die.
What he means:
I have a slight cold.

What he says:
Never.
What he means:
Not in the near future.

What he says:
I seduced her.
What he means:
She let me believe I seduced her.

What he says:
We got pretty intimate.
What he means:
She wouldn't let me sleep with her.

What he says:
Of course I'll dress smart.
What he means:
I'll wear matching socks – probably.

What he says:
I'm bi-curious.
What he means:
Tell me you fantasize about sleeping with women.

What he says:
I'm fine.
What he means:
I'm in extreme emotional pain.

What he says:
She's a real airhead.
What he means:
It should be easy to get her into bed.

What he says:
She's always getting angry.
What he means:
She displays more than one emotional state.

What he says:
She's constantly nagging.
What he means:
She expects me to pull my own weight.

What he says:
I apologise.
What he means:
I'm drunk/I don't want to talk about this anymore.

What he says:
She's a bitch at work.
What he means:
She has a normal amount of ambition.

What he says:
Please.
What he means:
I have absolutely no choice except death.

What he says:
She's far too assertive.
What he means:
She makes me doubt my own abilities.

What he says:
I love your back.
What he means:
It doesn't talk to me or look at me.

What he says:
I only called her a babe.
What he means:
Why can't women accept compliments?

What he says:
She's a real bitch.
What he means:
Doesn't she know women are supposed to be nicer than men.

What he says:
She's a real bimbo.
What he means:
She's perfect.

What he says:
She's a bit butch.
What he means:
Her hair is short and she has a healthy appetite.

What he says:
The room is tidy.
What he means:
It's possible to walk through the room.

What he says:
I am being clear.
What he means:
You must be stupid if you can't understand me.

What he says:
I am compassionate.
What he means:
I'll help anyone – as long as it's no trouble.

What he says:
She's always complaining.
What he means:
She has opinions.

What he says:
I can cook.
What he means:
I know how to make spaghetti wet and hot.

What he says:
Let's dance.
What he means:
I want to touch you without having to talk to you.

What he says:
Death doesn't scare me.
What he means:
Other people's death doesn't scare me.

What he says:
I'm on a diet.
What he means:
I'm thinking about cutting back on potato chips with my beer.

What he says:
I dressed up.
What he means:
I wore clothes that had been washed recently.

What he says:
She's evil.
What he means:
She's cheating on him – but not with me.

What he says:
She's spirited.
What he means:
She's cheating on him – with me.

What he says:
Everyone's doing it.
What he means:
People I would like to be like are doing it.

What he says:
She's an exhibitionist.
What he means:
She shows her body, but I don't want to see it.

What he says:
She's exotic.
What he means:
She's foreign and attractive.

What he says:
She's foreign.
What he means:
She's foreign and unattractive.

What he says:
Family.
What he means:
A bunch of people that keep me going to work so that I can give them enough to leave me in peace.

What he says:
Fear.
What he means:
The feeling that someone will learn too much about me.

What he says:
Perversity.
What he means:
Obsession with anything other than women's breasts, genitals, buttocks, foreign women in general, sport or fast cars.

What he says:
I forgive you.
What he means:
I'll pretend that I'm not still angry.

What he says:
I have my freedom.
What he means:
I am so deluded that I don't know I'm being controlled by women.

What he says:
She's a terrible flirt.
What he means:
She doesn't flirt with me.

What he says:
She's very warm and friendly.
What he means:
She flirts with me.

What he says:
She's a friend.
What he means:
I'd like to have sex with her one day.

What he says:
She's an old friend.
What he means:
She let me have sex with her once.

What he says:
The future.
What he means:
A time at which I have no idea what my feelings will be.

What he says:
The past.
What he means:
A time at which I can't remember what my feelings were.

What he says:
The present.
What he means:
A time at which my feelings don't matter.

What he says:
Gender-neutral.
What he means:
Homosexual.

What he says:
Homosexual.
What he means:
A man to be feared because he may find you attractive – or may not.

What he says:
I'm a gentleman.
What he means:
I'll open a door for a woman if I think there's a chance of getting her into bed or if I want to see her from behind.

What he says:
She's very graceful.
What he means:
She's thin.

What he says:
I feel guilty.
What he means:
I'm afraid I might get caught.

What he says:
I'm just a regular guy.
What he means:
I am profoundly mentally disturbed.

What he says:
I hate him.
What he means:
He thinks he's better than me – and so do I.

What he says:
She's too vain.
What he means:
She looks at herself more than she looks at me.

What he says:
Honesty.
What he means:
Something to be avoided at all costs.

What he says:
I'm only human.
What he means:
I have the instincts of a primitive ape, but am able to
pretend otherwise.

What he says:
She's hysterical.
What he means:
She won't believe that I'm always right.

What he says:
You must be insane.
What he means:
You saw right through me.

What he says:
Hi babe.
What he means:
Hello, I can't remember your name.

What he says:
Illicit.
What he means:
Fun without responsibility.

What he says:
I think I love her.
What he means:
I'm infatuated with her after one date.

What he says:
I can't put it into words.
What he means:
If I did put it into words you'd be so shocked you may scream.

What he says:
Indecent.
What he means:
Male nudity in public.

What he says:
Let me interpret that for you.
What he means:
Let me pretend I said something completely different.

What he says:
Intuition.
What he means:
The kind of random guessing that women are keen on.

What he says:
It was incredibly funny.
What he means:
Somebody else got hurt.

What he says:
You should think before you act.
What he means:
You should ask me before you act.

What he says:
I'm the jealous type.
What he means:
I wish she didn't have a mind of her own.

What he says:
I'm only looking for justice.
What he means:
I'm only looking for revenge.

What he says:
Kiss.
What he means:
A necessary prelude to the real point of the evening.

What he says:
She's a real lady.
What he means:
She won't slap you if you hold a door open for her.

What he says:
She's a lesbian.
What he means:
She doesn't pay me any attention.

What he says:
I'm lonely.
What he means:
I need sex.

What he says:
Love.
What he means:
To like a lot.

What he says:
I think make-up is a deception.
What he means:
. . .Which I will put up with if she needs it.

What he says:
Mirror.
What he means:
A useful source of information about my appearance that doesn't have opinions.

What he says:
Mother.
What he means:
A woman who is always convinced something is wrong with me.

What he says:
That didn't hurt.
What he means:
If I tell you what hurts me you may do it again.

What he says:
Why can't you be patient?
What he means:
I don't want to give you what you want.

What he says:
Why can't you be more active?
What he means:
I'm impatient.

What he says:
Relationship.
What he means:
Something she may try and slip into the conversation
without me noticing.

What he says:
Romance.
What he means:
Something I have to resort to when the straightforward
approach fails.

What he says:
Revenge.
What he means:
Getting a woman better looking than the one who dumped
me.

What he says:
She's too self-absorbed.
What he means:
She won't listen to me drone on for three hours about football.

What he says:
She's selfish.
What he means:
She's made sacrifices for me but expects me to do the same for her.

What he says:
Shopping.
What he means:
Only necessary when I run out of beer or the holes in my underwear join up.

What he says:
Smile.
What he means:
A facial expression necessary to prevent attractive women
from screaming when I meet them for the first time.

What he says:
Telephone.
What he means:
A good way to seem like you are staying in touch while
actually avoiding someone.

What he says:
I'm bored.
What he means:
Let's have sex.

What he says:
Nice dress!
What he means:
Nice cleavage!

What he says:
I love you
What he means:
Let's have sex now

What he says:
I love you, too!
What he means:
OK, I said it . . . NOW let's have sex.

What he says:
Yes, I like your new hairstyle.
What he means:
I liked it better before.

What he says:
That blouse and skirt don't go together.
What he means:
I'm gay.

What he says:
Was it good for you?
What he means:
I'm insecure about my manhood.

What he says:
I have something to tell you.
What he means:
Go and get tested.

What he says:
I've learned a lot from you.
What he means:
Next!!

What he says:
I want you back.
What he means:
I can't get a date.

What he says:
That's women's work.
What he means:
It's difficult, dirty and thankless.

What he says:
Yes, I heard you.
What he means:
I haven't any idea what you said.

What he says:
Presents don't prove my love.
What he means:
I forgot our anniversary again.

What he says:
My wife doesn't understand me.
What he means:
She actually expects me to talk to her.

What he says:
Go and ask your mother.
What he means:
I'm incapable of a decision about that.

What he says:
She's one of those rabid feminists.
What he means:
She refused to make my coffee.

What he says:
Going to stop off for a quick one.
What he means:
I'm going to drink myself into a stupor.

What he says:
I could never love anyone else.
What he means:
I'm used to the way you yell and nag.

What She Means vs What He Means

Men and women may use the same words – but actually be speaking a completely different language. Below is a new kind of dictionary to help you interpret . . .

Abandon
What she means: To totally give in to an emotion.
What he means: To cause someone pain by simply doing what you want.

Accessory
What she means: An essential addition to an outfit, e.g. a handbag or scarf.
What he means: To assist in a criminal act.

Abuse
What she means: Causing pain with words.
What he means: Causing pain with fists.

Accommodating
What she means: Pandering to the needs of others.
What he means: Pandering to the needs of people you can't beat up.

Accuse
What she means: To tell someone they have done something when they haven't, causing them to go out and do it immediately.
What he means: To tell someone they have done something when they haven't so that your own actions don't seem so bad.

Ache
What she means: A throbbing pain often caused by love.
What he means: A serious pain you couldn't possibly talk about.

Acquaintance
What she means: Someone you know but don't like.
What he means: Someone you don't have to pretend to feel about when something bad happens to them, e.g. death.

Action
What she means: Last resort when words get you nowhere.
What he means: Speaks louder than words.

Admit
What she means: To tell yourself or others the truth after a period of pretending you don't know the truth.
What he means: To let someone into your house or car.

Advantage
What she means: An inherent feature that makes you superior, e.g. a perfect waistline.
What he means: A temporary state of affairs that lets you win.

Afford
What she means: To have so much of something that you can give it away.
What he means: To be able to buy stuff.

Aggressive
What she means: Likely to start a fight.
What he means: Going for what you want despite the fear of failure.

Alone
What she means: When no one who understands you is nearby.
What he means: When no one is nearby.

Ambition
What she means: To have aspirations that are best not mentioned.
What he means: To have the will to get ahead.

Angst
What she means: Intense dread or fear.
What he means: Trendy word for nervous and foreign.

Apologize
What she means: To admit a mistake on the understanding that the other party will also admit their mistake.
What he means: To end an argument with minimum loss.

Ask
What she means: To wonder about something until someone gives it to you as a present or explains it fifteen times.
What he means: To sacrifice power and control, e.g. "Do you know where Maple Avenue is?"

Bald
What she means: Without disguise.
What he means: Without hair or protection.

Bar
What she means: A place to meet people who have no idea how repellent they are.
What he means: A place to stare at women and get drunk.

Basic
What she means: Essential or black.
What he means: A thing that is obvious to everyone except women and idiots.

Beauty
What she means: A goal only achievable through considerable pain.
What he means: Something pleasing to the senses.

Big
What she means: A word that, used correctly, can give you special powers over men.
What he means: What some parts of your body should be and others shouldn't be.

Better
What she means: What all women need to be before they are noticed.
What he means: Improved quality, usually through improved quantity.

Block
What she means: Emotional difficulties that have to be overcome.
What he means: Hard things useful for putting a car on.

Boast
What she means: To alienate people by speaking highly of yourself.
What he means: To impress and intimidate people by speaking highly of yourself.

Boyfriend
What she means: A man who calls on a regular basis and is an almost all-purpose companion.
What he means: A man who has exclusive rights to a particular woman for an unspecified period of time.

Break-up
What she means: An unpleasant process during which you cause pain to another in order to prevent pain being caused to you.
What he means: A process which is best carried out at the greatest emotional distance possible, e.g. by fax.

Bride
What she means: A woman who is the centre of attention for a few hours, usually for the first and only time in her life.
What he means: What your girlfriend can turn into if you are not careful.

Busy
What she means: No time for anything other than a serious phone call.
What he means: No time for anything other than a serious natural disaster e.g. earthquake.

Call
What she means: A proclamation of desire or friendship.
What he means: What you should do a few days after sex if you want it again.

Charm
What she means: To pretend successfully that there is nothing wrong with you.
What he means: When applied to women it means beautiful, when applied to men it means annoying.

Children
What she means: People to be idealized and loved above all others.
What he means: Small people with big appetites.

Close
What she means: Emotionally adjacent.
What he means: To shut.

Closet
What she means: Place to store clothing.
What he means: Place to store stuff of any kind.

Cohabit
What she means: To lose closet space and save on phone bills.
What he means: To gain exclusive rights with the option to buy later.

Commitment
What she means: When you know his shoe size and don't mind.
What he means: A way of saying "marriage" without actually saying "marriage".

Compassion
What she means: Generosity towards those you love or merely understand.
What he means: Generosity towards somebody that may be of use later.

Complain
What she means: The therapeutic action of announcing your problems to anyone who will listen.
What he means: To moan.

Complex
What she means: Emotionally difficult or complicated.
What he means: A big building such as a sports hall or military base.

Confront
What she means: To tell the truth at the risk of people disliking you.
What he means: To tell someone they have been caught doing something wrong.

Consent
What she means: To say that its okay to do something even when it's obvious that you agree.
What he means: To say yes.

Convert
What she means: To persuade someone that your way of thinking is right.
What he means: To adopt a new way of thinking due to logic, bribery or threats.

Cruel
What she means: Unforgivably mean behaviour.
What he means: Whatever makes her cry.

Cry
What she means: An expression of emotion.
What he means: An expression of emotion forbidden most of the time but expected during certain movies.

Date
What she means: An arranged day to get married.
What he means: The socially accepted way to get a woman alone.

Dear
What she means: A term of endearment.
What he means: A safe alternative if you have temporarily forgotten a woman's name.

Deceive
What she means: Not to tell someone when they believe something that is wrong.
What he means: To pretend you believe something when you don't.

Definite
What she means: Absolutely sure of something.
What he means: The opposite of annoying.

Demonstrate
What she means: To persuade by example.
What he means: To prove with diagrams.

Detachment
What she means: The act of cutting off emotion to avoid pain.
What he means: The act of keeping emotion under strict control.

Direct
What she means: Explicit, clear and ultimately boring.
What he means: To control something, e.g. he directed a movie blockbuster,

Dishonesty
What she means: To tell partial truths.
What he means: To lie.

Divert
What she means: To entertain or help someone by distracting their attention.
What he means: To turn something away from where it wants to go.

Drive
What she means: Ambition.
What he means: To hit hard, e.g. a golf ball.

Eager
What she means: Impatient for something to happen.
What he means: To be excited about something that may not happen.

Eligible
What she means: An unmarried man who does exciting things and is emotionally stable.
What he means: A woman who flirts.

Encourage
What she means: To make someone keep doing something by not rejecting him.
What he means: To ensure that someone keeps doing something you like.

Exercise
What she means: Activity intended to make parts of your body smaller.
What he means: Activity intended to make parts of your body larger.

Exotic
What she means: A far away place to take a vacation in.
What he means: A type of dancer.

Experience
What she means: Ineffective source of knowledge despite what people say.
What he means: Whatever you live through.

Failure
What she means: Inability to communicate.
What he means: Inability to get the job done.

Fashion
What she means: The ultimate and ever present expression of personality.
What he means: To make something, e.g. a club from a tree branch.

Feelings
What she means: The essential guidelines of the heart.
What he means: The annoying distractions of the heart.

First date
What she means: The first encounter; an information gathering exercise.
What he means: An audition; the first attempt.

Flimsy
What she means: Easily seen through, e.g. an excuse.
What he means: Easily got around, e.g. certain kinds of underwear.

Food
What she means: A source of obsession, comfort and calories.
What he means: A source of sustenance.

Frustration
What she means: Realizing not everyone shares your view of things.
What he means: Realizing you can't get what you want.

Game
What she means: A kind of entertainment.
What he means: A way of finding out who is best.

Get
What she means: To purchase or understand.
What he means: To obtain, e.g. to grab.

Guess
What she means: To find out you know more than you thought you did.
What he means: To pretend you know more than you do.

Gullible
What she means: Sensitive and impressionable.
What he means: Overly prone to trusting.

Hairstyle
What she means: A state to be changed constantly.
What he means: Another name for a haircut.

Hand holding
What she means: A sign of regard and trust.
What he means: Helping someone do something they should be able to do on their own.

Health
What she means: Physical strength and soundness.
What he means: The absence of disease.

Heroine
What she means: A woman whose sacrifices are, at least partially, noticed.
What he means: A woman who other women look up to.

Hold
What she means: To grasp tightly and not want to let go.
What he means: To temporarily not speak to someone, e.g. "I'm just putting you on hold".

Hug
What she means: To get close to someone.
What he means: To get close to something, e.g. a corner or a kerb.

Ignore
What she means: To make someone go away by not speaking to them; rarely effective.
What he means: To refuse interaction.

Impress
What she means: To put your best attributes on display.
What he means: To make people admire you.

Insult
What she means: To attack verbally, especially the target's favourite quality.
What he means: A form of humour or a method of starting a fist fight.

Intuition
What she means: Inner sense or vision.
What he means: Another word for guess.

Judgement
What she means: A vital quality that suffers in the presence of love.
What he means: A vital quality that suffers in the presence of naked flesh or alcohol.

Kill
What she means: To end the life of a living thing.
What he means: To put something beyond reach.

Language
What she means: A system of communication that sets humanity apart from animals.
What he means: A system of communication that allows you to get people to do what you want them to do.

Life
What she means: A series of difficult choices.
What he means: A series of difficult challenges.

Like
What she means: To love a bit.
What he means: Similar to.

Listen
What she means: To hear and care about what you are hearing.
What he means: To sit still and not speak while looking in the speaker's general direction.

Message
What she means: An important form of communication that can say nothing or everything.
What he means: A form of communication that you don't need to do anything about for a while.

Mistake
What she means: An educational experience.
What he means: An error.

Now
What she means: At any time in the next thirty to forty-five minutes.
What he means: At the present moment.

Outfit
What she means: An intelligent and powerful combination of clothes.
What he means: A military or industrial group.

Pack
What she means: To place everything you own in a series of suitcases before taking a vacation.
What he means: To carry a hidden weapon.

Perform
What she means: To do something impressive on a regular basis.
What he means: What it is essential to be able to do at all times.

Plan
What she means: Vision of what the future should be like.
What he means: Way to achieve something you want.

Problem
What she means: Difficulties to be talked about.
What he means: Difficulties to be removed or overcome.

Public
What she means: A place where you have to be even nicer than usual.
What he means: A place where you can do few of the things that you really like to do and that come naturally to you, e.g. urinating.

Question
What she means: The best way of phrasing almost anything, especially if you already know the answer.
What he means: A way of avoiding clear, useful, directness.

Read
What she means: To take in all aspects of something.
What he means: To appraise something for weaknesses.

Response
What she means: An answer that comes after carefully listening to a question.
What he means: An answer that shows that you are aware a question has been asked recently.

Rings
What she means: Finger jewellery with special qualities.
What he means: What a phone does.

Run
What she means: A serious and persistent design fault in tights.
What he means: Moving quickly, usually expected to be toward things, e.g. goals, enemy troops.

Sacrifice
What she means: To give up everything for someone you love or think you love.
What he means: To give up something in order to gain something else.

Self-esteem
What she means: Your inner sense of worth, determined by others' opinions.
What he means: Your inner sense of worth, determined by your power over others.

Silence
What she means: When you can't think of anything good to say.
What he means: Desirable at night, during certain TV shows, mornings and quite a lot of other times too.

Soon
What she means: Whenever you feel like doing something.
What he means: Before next week.
Stupid

What she means: Unable to understand basic human needs.
What he means: Unintelligent; likely to do something detrimental to the self.

Surrender
What she means: To give in to strong emotions and let them carry you where they will.
What he means: To lose or give up to an enemy.

Tact
What she means: Not telling people how truly awful or mistaken they are, even if it would be to their advantage.
What he means: Not asking basically stupid questions.

Talk
What she means: To make yourself feel better.
What he means: To fill in the time before action is taken.

Think
What she means: To freely associate ideas.
What he means: To mentally construct logical plans or reasons.

Tie
What she means: An emotional bond.
What he means: An unsatisfactory state in which nobody has won.

Unbelievable
What she means: Something wonderful because it could not have happened.
What he means: Something infuriating because it should not have occurred.

Unequal
What she means: An unbalanced relationship.
What he means: Where one person has more than another.

Vacation
What she means: A time that can be spent with loved ones or friends.
What he means: A time to get away from work.

Vulnerable
What she means: Being soft and demanding protection.
What he means: Weak and easy to hurt or beat.

Work
What she means: To carry out a task until somebody notices.
What he means: To carry out a task until it is finished.

Yes
What she means: No
What he means: Yes

CHAPTER 6

Sweet Revenge

The Joke's On Him

Men hate to be laughed at, so here's your chance for some sweet revenge. Enjoy this collection of jokes, insults and wise words about men and masculinity.

Men are great! Every woman should own one!!!

He's carrying on a great love affair – unassisted.

The reason why our bras don't always match our outfit is because we actually change our underwear.

Men would like monogamy better if it sounded less like monotony.

If you must grunt in reply, please develop a system to indicate a positive vs a negative grunt.

Men approve of premarital sex . . . until daughters are born.

His head is getting too big for his toupee.

Why is psychoanalysis quicker for a man than for a woman?
When it's time to go back to childhood, he's already there.

If women are a pain in the ass, men are a pain
EVERYWHERE!

Why do men name their penises?
Because they want to be on a first-name basis with the one
who makes all their decisions.

Men do come with instructions, they're just written in pig
Latin.

All men would really like to own a train set.

Men are like bras; they offer light, medium and complete
support.

We don't mind if you look in the mirror to check your appearance – in fact, please do!!!

His wife worships him – and so does he.

The more you think of him the less you think of him.

Why don't most men show their true feelings?
Because they don't have any.

Men are just like computers, and a smart woman keeps a backup.

His ego is the only thing that keeps on growing without nourishment.

Women dream of world peace, a safe environment and eliminating hunger . . .
Men dream of being stuck in an elevator with the Playboy Triplets.

He makes you wish birth control could be retroactive.

Men hate self-service. It's always so bad – and slow too.

Why is it so hard for women to find men who are sensitive, caring and good-looking?
Because they already have boyfriends.

Why do men like masturbation?
Because it's sex with someone they love.

He lights up a room when he leaves it.

Men are like fires; they go out if unattended.

What would get a man to always put the toilet seat down?
A sex-change operation.

Men play the game. Women know the score.

Man: Hey, gorgeous, how do you fancy a good time?
Woman: Sorry, I don't date outside my species.

Most men are halfway through life before they realize it's a do-it-yourself thing.

He's a pain in the neck, and some people have even a lower opinion of him.

Is your husband a bookworm?
No, just an ordinary one.

Men are only good for one thing . . . two, if they're good at it.

He never opens his mouth unless he has nothing to say.

How do men exercise at the beach?
They suck in their stomachs every time they see a bikini.

Men read *Playboy* for the articles like women go to the shopping malls for the music.

When all is said and done, he just keeps talking.

What does a man consider to be a seven-course meal?
A hot dog and a six pack.

Men and women were created equal, but women continued to improve.

A man sees a kiss as an application for a better position.

Men come in three sizes: small, medium and Ooohhh yesss!

What is gross stupidity?
144 men in one room.

He'd be better company if his mind worked as fast as his mouth.

We all spring from monkeys, but he didn't spring far enough.

Why do men like BMWs?
They can spell it.

A lot of men define marriage as a way to get maid service for free.

What's the difference between a single, 40-year-old woman and a single, 40-year-old man?
The woman thinks often of having children and the man thinks often about dating them.

What should you give to the man who has everything?
A   A woman to show him how to work it.
B   Penicillin.

Men don't care what's on TV. They only care what else is on TV

There's nothing wrong with him that reincarnation won't cure.

Why do black widow spiders kill the males after mating?
To stop the snoring before it starts.

When a man opens the door of his car for his wife, you can be sure of one thing: either the car is new or the wife.

Why don't men have mid-life crises?
They get stuck in adolescence.

He's dark and handsome; when it's dark, he's handsome.

He's not really his own worst enemy – not while anyone who has anything to do with him is still living.

Man: I enjoyed your book, who wrote it for you?
Woman: Darling, I'm so glad you liked it. Who read it to you?

What do you have when you have two little balls in your hand? A man's undivided attention.

At first, women think most men are the strong, silent type . . .
But then they realize that men have nothing to say.

When men insist that women are illogical . . .
Most times it's because the woman doesn't agree with them.

Men are always ready to respect anything that bores them.

Before marriage, a man will like awake all night thinking about something his lover says. After marriage, he'll fall asleep before his wife finishes . . .

Men like to barbecue. Men will cook if danger is involved.

Husband: Want a quickie?
Wife: As opposed to what?

How can a woman find out what life's like without a man around?
Get married.

He's the kind of man you just have to look at twice. The first time you don't believe it.

Marrying a divorced man is ecologically responsible. In a world where there are more women than men, it pays to recycle.

There's no point in asking him to behave like a human being – he doesn't do imitations.

Men like phones with lots of buttons. It makes them feel important.

All men are afraid of eyelash curlers – sleep with one under your pillow as an added deterrent.

What's the difference between a Porsche and a hedgehog? The hedgehog has pricks on the outside.

No wonder it's so difficult for a woman to establish a relationship . . .
Most men would rather pledge allegiance to a flag than to a woman.

What's the one thing that all men at singles bars have in common?
They're married.

Before money was invented . . .
What did women find attractive about men?

He has the kind of face you don't want to remember and just can't forget.

A good place to meet a man is at the dry cleaner. These men usually have jobs and bathe.

Why were men given larger brains than dogs?
A: So they wouldn't hump women's legs at cocktail parties.
B: So they wouldn't stop to play with every other man they see when you take them round the block.

How was Colonel Sanders a typical male?
All he cared about were legs, breasts and thighs.

He combs his hair with a sponge.

How can you tell it's puppy love for a man?
He slobbers all over the woman.

Man: I don't know why you wear a bra; you've got nothing to put in it.
Woman: You wear briefs, don't you?

What's easier to make, a snowman or a snowwoman?
A snowwoman is easier to make, because with a snowman you have to hollow out the head and use all that extra snow to make its testicles.

How is being at the singles bar different from going to the circus?
At the circus the clowns don't talk.

Men!!! Give them an inch . . .
And they'll try to somehow add it to their own.

He's a man of polish – mostly around his head.

What do most men think Mutual Orgasm is?
An insurance company.

Men are sensitive in strange ways. If a man has built a fire
and the last log does not burn, he will take it personally.

A man can actually cater to a woman's need, so long as all
that she wants is to have sex, watch sports and bring him a
beer.

Why do men say such stupid things?
Men like to.

Why do men have to act like such idiots?
Well, men don't actually have to; it's because they enjoy it.
It's the old fashioned pride in a job well done that's missing
in so much of the world these days.

Who needs a man? My dog growls, my parrot swears, my
fireplace smokes, my cat slinks home in the early morning
and a doctor looks me over.

What does a woman have to do to keep a man interested?
Wear a perfume that smells like beer.

What is a man's view of safe sex?
A padded headboard.

How do men sort their laundry?
"Filthy" or "Filthy, but wearable".

They say that men only think about sex. That's not exactly true. They also care a lot about power, world domination, money, sports and beer.

What does a man notice most when he's at the beach with his girlfriend?
Every other woman there.

He has less hair to comb, but more face to wash.

Why do men always have to ogle other women?
Women ogle men as well. They're just better at not getting caught.
Women take one quick look and memorize it for later reference.
Since men lack this ability, they have to burn it into their memories.

My husband has a very easygoing nature – he's too heavy to run and too fat to fight.

A single man in his forties often has a problem finding women at his level of maturity. That's why he dates someone half his age.

What do you call a man with 99% of his brain missing?
Castrated.

I knew him when he had only one stomach and one chin.

How do you know if a man is lying?
His lips are moving.

Getting rid of a man without hurting his masculinity is a problem. "Get out!" and "I never want to see you again!" are more of a challenge to him. If you want to get rid of a man, try saying, "I love you . . . I want to marry you . . . I want to have your children." Sometimes they leave skidmarks.

What's the difference between a husband and a new dog?
A. A dog is always happy to see you.
B. A dog only takes a couple of months to train.

Men are self-confident because they grow up identifying with super-heroes. Women have bad self-images because they grow up identifying with Barbie.

Why is sleeping with a man like a soap opera?
Just when it's getting interesting, they're finished until next time.

She's not divorcing him because there's any other man in her life. It's just that she's determined that there will be.

That man's so mean, the only thing he'll share with you is a communicable disease.

Why are men like blenders?
You need one but you're not quite sure why.

Male menopause is a lot more fun than female menopause. With female menopause you put on weight and have hot flushes. With male menopause you get to date young girls and drive motorcycles.

What do you call a man with half a brain?
Gifted.

What's the difference between a man and a catfish?
One is a bottom-feeding scum-sucker and the other is a fish.

Why do only 10% of men make it to Heaven?
Because if they all went, it would be Hell!

Men are brave enough to go to war, but not brave enough to have a bikini wax.

How do men define a 50/50 relationship?
Women cook, men eat; women clean, men get dirty; women iron, men wrinkle.

Men don't get cellulite. Most women believe that for this reason alone, God might just be male.

He's past it now; his head makes dates that his body can't keep.

Man: Hey, baby, what's your sign?
Woman: Do Not Enter.

Why are men like popcorn?
They satisfy you, but only for a little while.

Not one man in any beer commercial has a beer belly.

What do you call an intelligent man in America?
A tourist.

Why do so many women fake orgasm?
Because so many men fake foreplay.

Men who can eat anything they want and not gain weight
should do it out of sight of women.

How is a man like a snowstorm?
Because you don't know when he's coming, how many
inches you'll get or how long it'll stay.

What's the difference between a bar and a clitoris?
Most men have no trouble finding a bar.

Men lie about their jobs, drive cars they can't afford, wear
toupees and loose shirts that hide their stomachs, and say
they want a "real" woman!

Why did God create man?
Because a vibrator can't mow the lawn.

How can men sit on their asses all day without moving?
Men have very powerful sets of sitting muscles developed
by evolution that enable them to sit for extended periods of
time without getting tired.

Why would women be better off if men treated them like cars?
At least then they'd get some attention every six months or 50,000 miles.

What's the thinnest book in the world?
"What Men know about Women".

Men will do anything except not fall asleep immediately after sex, tell women what's wrong when they ask, and ask for directions when lost.

Oozing charm from every pore
He oiled his way across the floor.

How are men like chocolates?
A. They never last long enough.
B. They always leave stains whenever they get hot.

Why do men prefer blondes?
Men always like intellectual company.

Lots of men are poor communicators – it's hard to drink
beer and talk at the same time.

That man treats all women as sequels.

All he asks of a women are two keys – to her heart and her apartment.

What makes men chase women they have no intention of marrying?
The same urge that makes dogs chase cars they have no intention of driving.

What did God say after creating man?
I can do better.

Why do men want to marry virgins?
They can't stand criticism.

How many men does it take to screw a light bulb?
A   One – men will screw anything.
B   One – men will screw up anything.
C   Five – one to actually do the screwing, four to listen to
    him brag about it.

Man: No woman ever made a fool of me.
Woman: Who did then?

How can you tell if a man is aroused?
He's breathing.

How can you tell if a man is happy?
Who cares?

Wife: I won the lottery! Five million pounds. Whoo-eee—
start packing!
Husband: That's great!!! What should I pack?
Wife: Whatever you want, just be out of the house by the
time I get there.

So far as he's concerned, love is just a passing fanny.

Why is a woman different from a PC?
A woman won't accept a $3^{1}/_{2}''$ floppy.

Why is a man different from a PC?
You only have to tell the PC once.

Behind every great woman is a man telling her she's ignoring him.

Do men and women really suit each other? Perhaps they should just live next door and visit now and again.

What do a clitoris, an anniversary and a toilet have in common?
Men always miss them.

He's like a modern dry cleaner – he works fast and leaves no ring.

How can you tell the difference between men's real gifts
and their guilt gifts?
Guilt gifts are nicer.

If you think the way to a man's heart is through his
stomach, you're aiming way too high.

What is a man's idea of foreplay?
A half hour of begging.

Why is it good that there are women astronauts?
Because if the crew gets lost in space, at least the women
will ask for directions.

Never trust a man who says he's the boss at home – he'll most likely lie about other things too.

What does a man call true love?
An erection.

Why do doctors slap babies' bottoms right after they're born?
To knock the penises off the smart ones.

What do you call a dead man?
Trustworthy.

He has submarine hands. You never know where they'll turn up next.

If you want a nice, gentle man, go for an overweight bald one – they try harder.

How is a man like the weather?
Nothing can be done to change either one of them.

What do you call a man who expects to have sex on the second date?
Slow.

Behind every great man is a puzzled woman.

Always go for younger men – you might as well, most men never mature anyway.

He acts as if he had just invented sex and can't wait to spread the idea around.

Men are all the same – they just have different faces so you can tell them apart.

Why do men buy electric lawnmowers?
So they can find their way back to the house.

How do men define insomnia?
Waking up every few days.

He can count only up to sex.

What's the difference between men and pigs?
Pigs don't turn into men when they get drunk!

Why don't men cook at home?
No one's invented a steak that will fit in the toaster.

Men are like animals – messy, insensitive and potentially violent, but occasionally make great pets.

What's the difference between men and government bonds?
Bonds mature.

Why are bankers good lovers?
Because they know first hand the penalty for early withdrawal.

Men's brains are like the prison system – not enough cells.

How does a woman know her man is cheating on her?
He starts showering twice a week.

What do you call a woman who works like a man?
Lazy.

There are only two four-letter words that are offensive to men – "don't" and "stop" (unless they're used together).

Why do men need instant replays on TV sports?
Because they've forgotten what happened after 30 seconds.

What is that insensitive bit at the base of the penis called?
The man.

How do you save a man from drowning?
Take your foot off his head.

Why is a man like a moped?
They're both fun to ride until your friends see you with one.

Husbands are like children – they're fine if they're
somebody else's.

What's the difference between a man and a parrot?
You can teach a parrot to talk nicely.

Did you hear about the woman who finally figured men out?
She died laughing before she could tell anybody.

Husband: This coffee isn't fit for a pig!
Wife: No problem, I'll get you some that is.

What do you get when you cross a man with a pig?
Nothing. There are some things even a pig won't do.

If a man appears sexy, caring and smart, give him a day or two – he'll soon be back to his usual self.

Why are men and spray paint alike?
One squeeze and they're all over you.

What's the difference between a marriage and a mental hospital?
At a mental hospital you have to show improvement to get out.

Why are men like laxatives?
They can irritate the **** out of you.

What's a man's definition of a romantic evening?
Sex.

Why don't men mind their own business?
A. No mind.
B. No business.

There *are* men who are sensitive, caring and good looking
– but they probably already have boyfriends.

What do men and women have in common?
They both distrust men.

Why do a married man and his single mate envy each other?
Each one thinks the other is having sex more often.

We try to keep him out of the kitchen.
Last time he cooked, he burned the salad.

What does a man notice most when he's with his girlfriend?
Every other woman around.

Men view life as a competition: if you're better than they are at something, they pretend it's not important.

What's the most effective birth control device for men?
Their manners.

Why do men have holes in the end of their penises?
So oxygen can get into their brains.

How many men does it take to change a roll of toilet paper?
Who knows – did it ever happen?

What's the only way to make sure your husband remembers
your anniversary?
Get married on his birthday.

Why are men like commercials?
You can't believe a word they say.

He threatened to divorce her once, and she couldn't help
shedding a few tears.

What's a sure sign a man is planning to be unfaithful?
If he has a penis.

When macho man finds himself unable to perform . . .
He'll ask the woman, "Does this happen to you often?"

Why are married women heavier than single women?
Single women come home, see what's in the refrigerator and go to bed.
Married women come home, see what's in bed and go to the refrigerator.

What do you instantly know about a well-dressed man?
His wife picked out his clothes.

What's the difference between a man and childbirth?
One can be terribly painful and sometimes almost unbearable, while the other is just having a baby.

He's very class conscious. He has no class and everyone is conscious of it.

Why do most men resist becoming fathers?
Because they aren't through being children yet.

What is a "successful hunting trip"?
When three men kill nine cases of Budweiser in two days.

Why don't men believe in paternity tests?
Because the sample is taken from their finger.

She's leaving her money to charity and her brains to him.

What do you do with a bachelor who thinks he's God's gift?
Exchange him.

How are men like noodles?
They're always in hot water, they lack taste and they need dough.

What's a man's idea of doing housework?
Lifting his legs so you can vacuum.

Men are proof of reincarnation.
You can't get that dumb in just one lifetime.

Wife, refusing to give her husband a divorce: I've suffered you for fifteen years, and now I should make you happy?

What's the difference between a man and a messy room?
You can straighten up a messy room.

These days, "The Rat Race" really means . . .
If there's one rat in a room full of men, he'll hit on you first.

What do you do if your best friend runs off with your husband?
Miss her.
Pity her.

He's a fellow of a few, ill-chosen words.

Men often go looking for sex and end up finding love . . . Women often go looking for love and end up finding only sex.

What's the difference between a man and E.T.?
E.T. phoned home.

He's supporting her in the manner to which she was accustomed – he's letting her keep her job.

He's a perfect gentleman. When she drops something, he kicks it to where she can pick it up easier.

Fortune teller: You'll be a widow soon . . . your husband will die by poisoning.
Woman: Will I be acquitted?

Why do bachelors like clever women?
Opposites attract.

He's a fellow of a few, ill-chosen words.

The only way he can live up to his ideal of himself is from a hole in the ground.

How do you get a man to do sit-ups?
Put the remote control between his toes.

Just before his birthday, her friends asked what she was
getting for him, and she said, "Make me an offer."

He's very considerate. He holds the door open for her when
she staggers in with the groceries.

How does a man save a woman from being attacked on the
street at night?
He controls himself.

They were married for better or for worse. He couldn't
have done better and she couldn't have done worse.

Why do men like blonde jokes so much? Because they can
understand them.

What's the difference between a man and Bigfoot?
One is covered with matted hair and smells awful. The
other has big feet.

He eats with his fingers and talks with his fork.

Why don't men like to drink coffee at work?
It keeps them awake.

All she wants is to see his name, just once, in the obituary column.

How do most men define marriage?
A very expensive way to get your laundry done free.

What's the quickest way to lose 190 pounds of ugly fat?
Divorce him.

Why do men come home drunk and leave their clothes on
the floor?
Because they're still in them.

Whoever said women can't take a joke obviously hasn't
seen her husband.

What's the difference between a man and an ox?
Fifteen pounds and a six-pack.

How many men would it take to mop a floor?
No one knows; they've never done it.

She thought she had a model husband; unfortunately he's not a working model.

We've all heard soup gargled and siphoned, but he yodels it.

He's a contact man – all con and no tact.

Why don't men do the laundry?
Because the washer and dryer don't run on remote control!

She'll never forget the first time they met, but she's trying hard.

Wife: Do you love me just because my father left me a fortune?
Husband: Not at all honey, I would love you no matter who left you the money.

What's the difference between an intelligent man and a UFO?
I don't know, I've never seen either.

He never paws a girl. His hands are too busy hanging on to his wallet.

What did God say after She made Eve?
"Practice makes perfect."

He keeps a record of everything he eats.
It's called a tie.

She married him for his money – and she's earning every penny of it.

What's the difference between a man and a cow?
One brain cell that prevents them from shitting all over the place.

Did you hear about the baby born with both sexes?
It had a penis AND a brain!

He takes his troubles like a man; he blames them on her.

Why are men like paper cups?
They're dispensable.

He has the manners of a gentleman. Obviously, they don't belong to him.

As they left the divorce court, she whispered to him: "Bye now – pay later."

Learn from the Experts

Comments, observations and sharp insights into the male psyche from well-known women who've played their part in the battle of the sexes.

Life after death is as improbable as sex after marriage
> Madelein Kahn

A husband is what's left of a lover, after the nerve has been extracted.
> Helen Rowland

The useless piece of flesh at the end of a penis is called a man.
> Jo Brand

Scratch a lover, and find a foe.
> Dorothy Parker

I don't like all-in wrestling – if it's all in, why wrestle?
　　Mae West

Ask him the time and he'll tell you how the watch was made.
　　　Jane Wyman (of ex-husband Ronald Reagan)

In Hollywood, marriage is a success if it outlives milk.
　　Rita Rudner

Foreplay is like beefburgers – three minutes each side.
　　Victoria Wood

The only way to get rid of cockroaches is to tell them you want a long term relationship.
> Jasmine Birtles

Why should women mind if men have their faces on the money as long as we have our hands on it?
> Ivy Priest

A hard man is good to find.
> Mae West

Women want mediocre men, and men are working hard to be as mediocre as possible.
> Margaret Mead

Never trust a husband too far, nor a bachelor too near.
    Helen Rowland

Let's forget the six feet and talk about the seven inches.
    Mae West

The only time a woman has a true orgasm is when she's shopping.
    Joan Rivers

Men are like car alarms – they both make a lot of noise no one listens to.
    Diana Jordan

You remind me of my brother – only he has a human head.
        Judy Tenuta.

Don't imagine you can change a man, unless he's in
nappies.
        Jasmine Birtles

The hardest task in a girl's life is to prove to a man that his
intentions are serious.
        Helen Rowland
Macho does not prove mucho.
        Zsa Zsa Gabor

I married beneath me. All women do.
        Nancy Astor

A man in the house is worth two in the street.
    Mae West

The feminine vanity case is the grave of masculine
illusions.
    Helen Rowland

Always suspect any job men willingly vacate for women.
    Jill Tweedie

No nice men are good at getting taxis.
    Katharine Whitehorn

Give a man a free hand and he'll run it all over you.
    Mae West

The male is a domestic animal which, if treated with
firmness and kindness, can be trained to do most things.
    Jilly Cooper

The only really masterful noise a man makes in the house is
the noise of his key, when he is still on the landing,
fumbling for the lock.
    Colette

Bloody men are like bloody buses
You wait for about a year
And as soon as one approaches your stop
Two or three others appear.
    Wendy Cope

A man . . . is so in the way in the house!
    Elizabeth Gaskell

Never let one man worry your mind. Find 'em, fool 'em
and forget 'em.
    Mae West

The more I see of men, the more I admire dogs.
    Marquise de Sévigné

I require only three things of a man: he must be handsome,
ruthless and stupid.
    Dorothy Parker

Women are never stronger than when they arm themselves
with their weaknesses.
Mme du Deffand

Whatever women do, they must do it twice as well as men
to be thought half as good. Luckily this is not difficult.
Charlotte Whitton

Scheherazade is the classic example of a woman saving her
head by using it.
Esme Wynne-Tyson

What's wrong with you men? Would hair stop growing on
your chest if you asked directions somewhere?
Erma Bombeck

Never despise what it says in the women's magazines: it may not be subtle but neither are men.
Zsa Zsa Gabor

If men could get pregnant, abortion would be a sacrament.
Florynce Kennedy

There are men I could spend eternity with. But not this life.
Kathleen Norris

Most women set out to try to change a man, and when they have changed him they do not like him.
Marlene Dietrich

More and more it appears that, biologically, men are designed for short, brutal lives and women for long, miserable ones.

        Estelle Ramey

Women must come off the pedestal. Men put us up there to get us out of the way.

        Viscountess Rhondda

A woman needs a man like a fish needs a bicycle.

        Gloria Steinem

Why are women so much more interesting to men than men are to women?

        Virginia Woolf

Make Him Mad
How to be the stereotypically annoying female

It's the little things that you say and do – so polish up those sharp retorts and practise that *really* irritating behaviour that's guaranteed to cause fireworks!

Do not say what you mean – EVER

Be ambiguous – always

"If I watch football with you, it's not bonding, it's the butts I'm looking at."

Cry – be inconsolable

"Don't insist that I 'get off the damn phone' and then not talk to me."

Bring things up that were said, done or thought years, months or decades ago.

"I don't care if you hold the remote – unlike you, however, I don't enjoy watching 27 seconds of 117 different programmes."

Bring things up that were done with other boyfriends or ex-partners.

Make them apologize for everything.

No, I'm not impressed with your car – it takes no special skills to make car payments each month.

Stash feminine products in their cars and backpacks. Leave notes in their books as cute reminders that you were thinking of them.

Look them in the eye and start laughing.

Please don't attempt to drive when you're not driving.

Get angry at them for everything.

Discuss your period in front of them – watch them squirm.

Demand to be called or e-mailed – often; whine when they don't comply.

My bedtime headaches are inversely proportional to the number of showers/baths you take.

When complimented, be sure to be paranoid.

Take nothing at face value.

Stop telling me most male strippers are gay – I don't care!

Be late for everything – yell if they're late.

Yes, I do look at other men. However, I don't drool like you do when you check out a "babe".

Talk about your ex's all the time – compare and contrast.

Your contributions to your children should go above and beyond that Y chromosome you unselfishly sacrificed.

Make them guess what you want and then get mad when they're wrong.

Plan little monthly relationship anniversaries.

Eye contact is best established above our shoulder-level.

Get mad at them if they forget monthly anniversaries – then cry.

Gather all your female friends and dance to *I will Survive* while they're present.

Some women actually know more about a car and the mechanics involved than you do.

Constantly claim you're fat – Ask them – Then cry, regardless of the answer.

Leave out the good parts in stories.

We go to the Ladies Room in groups to talk about you.

Whenever there is a silence, ask them, "What are you thinking about?"

Always make them wonder about everything – Confusion is a good thing.

Criticize the way they dress.

Criticize the music they listen to.

Criticize their friends.

If asked, "What's wrong?", tell them if they don't know, you're not going to tell them.

Try to change them.

Try to mould them.

Try to get them to dance.

When they screw up, never let them forget it.

Make them stay at religious services until they are close to fainting.

Use "Just because" as an answer frequently.

Blame everything on PMS.

Read something into everything.

Over-analyze everything.

Frighten Him

Feel like making him dazed, nervous and confused? Then try one (or all, if you're really serious!) of the FIVE QUESTIONS MOST FEARED BY MEN.
Remember, there is only ONE correct answer; incorrect answers should be severely punished. Think about your chosen responses to his incorrect answers *before* you begin and, with practice, you will enjoy many happy hours of explosive arguments which will ultimately ensure you get what you want.

THE FIVE QUESTIONS
1. What are you thinking about?
2. Do you love me?
3. Do I look fat?
4. Do you think she is prettier than me?
5. What would you do if I died?

QUESTION ONE

What are you thinking about?

Correct answer: "I'm sorry if I seemed far away, darling. I
was just reflecting on what a warm, wonderful,
thoughtful, caring, intelligent, beautiful woman you
are, and how lucky I am to have found you."

Incorrect answers (i.e. the truth) include:
1. Football.
2. Formula One.
3. How fat you are.
4. How much prettier she is than you.
5. How I would spend the insurance money if you died.

QUESTION TWO

Do you love me?

Correct answer: "Yes!" or, for extra emphasis, "Yes, dear!"

Incorrect answers include:
1. I suppose so.
2. Would it make you feel better if I said "yes"?
3. That depends on what you mean by love.
4. Does it matter?
5. Who, me?

QUESTION THREE

Do I look fat?

Correct answer: "Of course not!" (spoken emphatically and with conviction)

Incorrect answers include:
1. Compared to what?
2. I wouldn't call you fat, but you're not exactly thin either.
3. A little extra weight looks good on you.
4. I've seen fatter
5. What did you say? I was just thinking about how I would spend the insurance money if you died.

QUESTION FOUR

Do you think she's prettier than me?

Correct answer: "Of course not, you're much prettier!"

Incorrect answers include:
1. Yes, but you have a better personality.
2. Not prettier, just pretty in a different way.
3. Not as pretty as you when you were her age.
4. Only in the sense that she's thinner.
5. What did you say? I was just thinking about how I would spend the insurance money if you died.

QUESTION FIVE

What would you do if I died?

Correct answer: "I wouldn't want to carry on living without
   you, darling."

Incorrect answers include:
1. I'd have to find someone else – you know I can't cook.
2. Do you mean before or after the funeral?
3. Try to get over my grief with a week of non-stop sex.
4. Call the travel agent and plan a trip to the sun to get
   away from it all.
5. Call the insurance company.

Be Prepared!

**Be prepared for those put downs from him and work out
your response in advance. Luckily men are anything but
subtle – which means that with a little thought you can
easily turn the tables on him and puncture that over-
inflated ego with a sharp come-back.**

TYPICAL INSULTS AND OBSTRUCTIVE
BEHAVIOUR FROM HIM

Don't ask, OK?

No, we can't be friends I just want you for sex.

The dress doesn't make you look fat, it's the fact that you eat too much.

You've got no chance of me calling you – EVER!

No, I won't be gentle – where's the fun in that?

Well, yes, actually, I do this all the time.

I hate all your stupid friends.

I have every intention of using you . . . and none of even speaking to you after tonight.

Yes, I mind waiting very much . . . if you're not ready in five more minutes, forget it!

No, I would not rather talk than watch the game.

I don't care if you did spend all day cooking – it still tastes terrible!

Your hair looks as good as it's ever going to look – let's go!

No, I don't intend to do anything all day – it's a Sunday, a day of rest.

Yeah, we're lost – so what – enjoy the scenery.

No, I don't really care that you didn't climax too.

Because it's a neat new tool – that's why I bought it.

No, I don't want to go shopping with you – not now, not ever!

Yes, I certainly was staring at that girl's boobs.

Sure I was flirting . . . she looks like she'd be good in bed.

Yes, I know exactly how long the game's been on. There's a clock right there on the screen.

No, the *Playboy* channel wasn't included in the package – we pay extra for it.

Actually, I do find her a lot more attractive than you.

Yes, I do talk more than five minutes on the phone . . . not with you, however.

Because the more beer I drink, the less annoying you seem to be.

No, I don't think our marriage was a mistake – it was a disaster.

Because it's a wife's job – that's why!

You're right – I can't stand the kids.

No, actually, I didn't miss you at all; it was rather peaceful in fact.

Buy a Dog!

Still looking for something that's warm and cuddly, is always pleased to see you, responds to you affectionately and is sensitive to your moods? Then it just has to be a dog! There are, it must be said, a few advantages that men have over dogs but, on the whole, there are some very sound reasons why a dog could make your life much easier . . .

How Dogs and Men are Similar:

Both take up too much space on the bed.

Both have irrational fears about vacuum cleaners.

Both are threatened by their own kind.

Both mark and protect their territory.

Both are bad at making you understand what it is they want.

Neither can tell you what's bothering them.

The smaller ones tend to be more nervous.

Neither does any dishes or house cleaning.

Both are shamelessly smelly.

Neither of them notices when you get your hair cut.

Both like dominance games.

Both are suspicious of men who come to the door.

Neither knows how to talk on the telephone.

Both have obsessions about cats.

Both enjoy mindless games.

Why Dogs are Better than Men:

Dogs do not have problems expressing affection in public.

Dogs miss you when you're gone and greet you when you return.

Dogs feel guilty when they've done something wrong.

Dogs do not play mind games with you.

Dogs never laugh at how you throw.

Dogs do not feel threatened by your intelligence.

You can train a dog.

Dogs mean it when they kiss you.